D1611832

A NATURAL HISTORY OF THE COMMON LAW

JAMES S. CARPENTIER LECTURES

A NATURAL HISTORY OF THE COMMON LAW

S.F.C. MILSOM

COLUMBIA UNIVERSITY PRESS   NEW YORK

Columbia University Press
Publishers Since 1893
New York   Chichester, West Sussex
Copyright © 2003 Columbia University Press

Library of Congress Cataloging-in-Publication Data
Milsom, S. F. C. (Stroud Francis Charles), 1923–
   A natural history of the common law / S.F.C. Milsom.
      p.   cm.
   Includes bibliographical references and index.
   ISBN 978–0–231–12994–7 (alk. paper)
      1. Common law—England—History. 2. Common law—History.
   I. Title.

   KD671.M543 2003
   340.5'7'0942—dc21

                                                    2003048979

Printed in the United States of America

c 10 9 8 7 6 5

JAMES S. CARPENTIER LECTURES

CONTENTS

PREFACE

THESE ESSAYS SPRING ULTIMATELY FROM AN
interest addressed in lectures and articles over many years and immediately from an invitation to give the Carpentier lectures at the
law school of Columbia University in 1995. The first three essays
contain most of the substance of those lectures, though somewhat
enlarged and rearranged. The last essay is partly new and is concerned not so much with the mechanisms of legal development
and legal change as with the slippery nature of the evidence with
which legal historians have to deal.

I am deeply grateful to the dean and faculty of the Columbia
Law School for inviting me to give the lectures and for much
kindness and hospitality at the time. To Professor Barbara Black
I owe a further debt for her friendship and encouragement over
many years.

Perhaps I may be forgiven for one further acknowledgment
which in her lifetime my wife would never allow me to make: all
who knew us know how great my debt to her has been.

Bracton *Bracton de legibus et consuetudinibus Angliae*, edited by G. E. Woodbine (4 vols., Yale University Press, 1915–1942); photographically reproduced with facing-page translation and notes (in effect constituting a new edition) by S. E. Thorne (4 vols., Harvard University Press, 1968–1977). References are to the latter, referred to as "ed. Thorne." *Bracton* has to go into italics because Thorne's work made it clear that the man Bracton did not write the book any more than Glanvill wrote *Glanvill*.

Bracton's Note Book edited by F. W. Maitland (3 vols., Cambridge University Press, 1887). The connection with *Bracton* is problematical. References are to entry numbers, not page numbers (except where the reference is to one of Maitland's footnotes).

Curia Regis Rolls (Stationery Office, 1922–1991; Boydell, 1999–). For the first ten volumes reference are to page numbers, thereafter entry numbers.

Glanvill *Tractatus de legibus et consuetudinibus regni Anglie qui Glanvilla vocatur*, edited and translated by G. D. G. Hall (Nelson, 1965). This supersedes an edition without translation by G. E. Woodbine (Yale University Press, 1932) in which, however, the notes are sometimes useful.

Rotuli Curiae Regis   edited by F. Palgrave (2 vols., Record Commission, 1835). Only page numbers.

YB, YBB   Editions of some year books of Edward I and Edward III were produced for the Rolls Series (R.S.), those of Edward II by the Selden Society (for which volume numbers given are those of the regular annual Selden Society series, not those of its year books series). "Black-letter" references are to the older quarto volumes.

INTRODUCTION

THE JURIST, THE LAWYER LOOKING AT LAW FROM a distance, is a species extinct in the common-law world. His habitat was annexed by philosophers as a playground for their own games. The older kind of analytical jurisprudence was still worth scorning when the writer was young: but historical jurisprudence had been discredited too long before to attract even the contempt due to the beliefs of one's teachers. Anthropologists and sociologists may make general observations about law, but not lawyers. Comparative lawyers may juxtapose the responses of different societies to similar conditions, and legal historians may trace the responses of a single society to changing conditions. What you may not do is to make general statements about legal development or postulate properties for law itself.

But you can try; and these essays are such an attempt by one who turned reluctantly from natural science to the law and who could never quite suppress a hankering for test tubes. They will indulge the fancy that there may be legal as well as social and economic causes and effects, perhaps even that legal systems may pass through something like a life cycle. Of course it is largely a fancy. No process that depends upon people thinking can be reducible to scientific cause and effect, especially if there are many people thinking independently. And even if there are regularities in fact, we can hardly hope to see them. If it means anything to speak of a life cycle, for example, only two systems in the Western world have lived through it; for the Roman system there are no more than scraps of evidence until it had reached a stage in the second century A.D. which seems to be comparable with the common-law system in the eighteenth.[1] By then the English system had been preserving court records for some six centuries, and for five of them had also been keeping notes of actual discussions in court. Early examples of those notes prompted the greatest of English legal historians to write: "A stage in the history of jurisprudence is here pictured for us, photographed for us, in minute detail. The parallel stage in the history of Roman law is represented, and can only be represented, by ingenious guess-work: acute and cautious it may be, but it is guess-work still."[2]

For the well-being of English legal history, I believe that this insight of Maitland's came to him too late. It came in its full force only when he turned to editing court reports of the early fourteenth century, and that was after his most influential work had been published.[3] His *History of English Law* (down to 1272) established both the subject and the assumptions on which historians have worked ever since; and ironically it had been based on the thirteenth-century book known as *Bracton*, which was infected by Roman ideas and Roman legal language. The infection was only of the skin, but the skin is what you see. Borrowed book learning in *Bracton* made its English law appear on the surface to be of the same nature as the developed Roman law, and Maitland's great book fostered that assumption. If it ever became explicit in his mind, he may have been puzzled by the "stage in the history of jurisprudence" that he later saw in the early yearbook reports. These were after *Bracton* in time, yet he expressly identified them with a stage in the Roman development so early that guesswork must stand in for evidence.

There is of course no doubt about the chronology: *Bracton* did come before the year books. The men behind that baffling work had, as it were, opened a time capsule and absorbed the perceptions of a legal culture which in an earlier civilization had passed through the cycle from infancy to maturity (and on to decadence).[4] They could think of law, as we do, as an intellectually coherent system of substantive rules that courts would bring to bear on the particular facts of each case. In their own church courts, indeed, they applied a system derived from the Roman; and those courts had judges armed with law-books and with mechanisms for ascertaining the facts to which the law would be applied.[5]

The pattern was unrecognizably different in the regular English lay courts which were at the beginning of the cycle. Lawsuits settled most kinds of dispute without finding the facts, let alone analyzing them; and the questions which substantive rules would one day answer had yet to be asked. Inflexible claim would be met by inflexible denial; one side or the other would swear an equally inflexible oath; and that oath would be put to supernatural test. The formula of claim would of course make some standard factual allegation; and in the relatively rare cases in which the claimant or another could affirmatively swear to that allegation and "prove" his oath by battle, the fact alleged was in some sense in issue. But by far the commonest oath tested was a defendant's oath of denial, and the denial was not of any past facts alleged in the claim but of present liability. There was no stage in that kind of lawsuit at which the Roman learning could be brought to bear; and the first of these essays, starting from a graphic illustration of that point, will seek to trace the devious and slow means by which in England legal questions came to be asked and answered.

But the explicit rule that answers today's question will become an obstacle to the reasonable needs of tomorrow. Obstacles can be removed or got round. The former is an openly deliberate process; and in our own time we think of adjustment by legislation as something obvious and wonder (too often with pity or contempt) why change had to come about by the kind of convolution to be considered in the second of these essays, why straightforward legislative adjustment of most private law comes so late. But legal thinking was not in terms of a system of substantive rules which a legislative mind might view, as it were, from above. There was no legislative mind, no view from above, no substantive law to be viewed, not even much of a system. Legal thinking was about the procedural possibilities open to individual lawyers in a world of intellectual free enterprise, and the convolutions were not intended to change "the law" or indeed intended at all: they were the cumulative residue of innumerable tiny twists, each intended only to serve the client of the day. The result of those twists, since without legislation you cannot change even procedural answers, was to change the questions. Disputes came to be brought within different compartments of the law, tort rather than contract or (perhaps partly because thinking in terms of such clear categories became untenable) one "form of action" rather than another.

The largest difficulty in legal history is precisely that we look at past evidence in the light of later assumptions, including our own assumptions about the nature and working of law itself. If before the nineteenth century we do not find the law about obligations being reduced to substantive statement in textbooks, or substantive change being made by legislation (or people suggesting that these two things might be combined in statutory codes), that is not because lawyers were lazy or unenterprising. In the areas we should identify as contract and tort (and up to a point crime) they were still thinking in procedural rather than substantive terms. But things were very different with property law. In Littleton's *Tenures* we have what can reasonably be called a textbook of land law as early as the fifteenth century, itself based on yet earlier work; and legislation was making changes (and causing larger ones) as early as the twelfth and thirteenth centuries. The processes by which this area of law was made and changed were quite different from those at work with obligations, and those different processes, particularly the transforming effect of a superior jurisdiction, will be examined in the third of these essays.

A part of that discussion, however, will be carried over as illustrating a main theme of the fourth and last essay. That will be concerned not with legal development or legal change for their own sakes but with why those processes can be so hard for the historian to see, why the evidence can be so fundamentally ambiguous. And this introduction must return to the autobiography with which it began. The would-be scientist who turned to the law and its history has more than once found himself making elementary propositions which are irreconcilable with the received learning and either obvious or wrong, but hardly capable of proof either way. Since at best there may be scraps of direct evidence for small corollaries, the first reaction has been to dismiss the propositions as wrong and the writer as a serial heretic; and he has almost wondered whether this was some quality peculiar to himself, wished upon him by a malign fairy godmother. But with legal history, as sometimes with the natural sciences, truly elementary propositions may stand or fall not with evidence of particular facts but with their power to explain all the facts; and the last of these essays will seek to explain why that should be so.

Two things follow. First, the last essay will inevitably refer to factual material considered in earlier essays. Second, these essays will be autobiographical in another sense. The factual material will be taken from topics on which the writer has spent much of his working life. He can only hope that he will not be taken as just recycling old propositions or just refighting old battles for their own sakes. Right or wrong, the general propositions of these essays have grown from those old particular battles and could not have been made in terms of materials less than totally familiar.

————

Autobiography provokes speculation of a different kind. If one can think of a natural history of law, can one think also of a natural history of legal history? That the thinking of any kind of historian must be limited by the world in which he lives is a truism it is not easy to keep in mind. At the turn of the nineteenth and twentieth centuries, for example, it would have been hard for anyone on either side of the Atlantic to suppose that the common law of property in land could possibly have grown from a "feudal" structure—that the secure landowner could have developed from one who was truly a tenant, in principle holding by the determinable allocation of an authority which, in this respect at least, was sovereign. Perhaps bizarrely, it may have been the model of the socialist systems of law that brought the possibility within range of twentieth-century imagination. But that of course is an observation only of hindsight: the model may have made the thought thinkable, but it did not suggest it.

The thought suggests another. How could a tenant whose tenure was somehow conditional have turned into an unconditional owner? Again without imagining any conscious linkage, there was in twentieth-century England the model of a transformation similar in principle though on a much smaller scale. Leaving aside the affluent minority, most households lived in rented accommodation held on short-term periodic leases; so there was nothing to stop landlords raising rents to whatever the market would bear and nothing to protect tenants against consequential eviction. Legislation during the First World War protected the families of soldiers and sailors by fixing the rents that landlords could demand for most small dwellings, and this system became so deeply embedded in society that it long outlived its original purpose. The consequence, undesired but seemingly unstoppable, was that protected tenancies became a new kind of property which could be bought and sold.[6] They regularly changed hands for (theoretically illicit) "key money," which represented some of the difference between the controlled rent and the market value. The economic reality of a relationship had been largely reversed by external control; and readers who persevere as far as the last two of these essays may see an analogy with much larger changes in the twelfth and thirteenth centuries.

If the historian's vision of the past is largely limited by the conditions of his own time, how far may it be affected by the course of his own life? Can one think there may be a natural history not just of legal history but of the individual legal historian? To borrow useful jargon, does it matter where he is coming from? It certainly matters whether he is coming from law or history. Maitland was a very accomplished if not very successful barrister before he became a law teacher, and he was clear in his belief that one needed a legal background to do good work in legal history.[7] At the time this seemed obvious enough, and it still does to some, particularly those who like the writer came to legal history from the law. But half a century later a nonlegal historian took prim offense, actually feeling entitled to explain Maitland's statement away as an aberration due to illness.[8]

This was Theodore Plucknett, a pure historian who, guided by a lawyer, wrote a Cambridge dissertation for what would now be the Ph.D. but which then gained him the degree of LL.B.[9] Those letters after his name no doubt played a part in the improbable course his life was to take. Going to Harvard on a traveling fellowship, Plucknett was engaged by Roscoe Pound to teach a legal history course in the law school, and some years (and a remarkable book) later a chair of legal history was created for him in the law department of the London School of Economics. So the historian who knew no law (and hardly ever even talked with his lawyer colleagues) spent his life teaching legal history to law students. He did much valuable work in many areas, mostly those on the institutional and social boundaries of the law. But truly legal questions could pass him unrecognized, and examples will be mentioned later in these essays.[10]

This is not just a turf war between two academic disciplines, not a simple question of who owns this sector of the past. There are large differences of approach. One is almost mechanical. For half a century and more nonlegal historians have narrowed their field of vision, increasingly dealing with smaller topics in shorter periods, and even their indexes, largely or wholly confined to names and places, show a shift in interest from the general to the particular. That is a shift the legal historian cannot make. The law consists of generalizations (and ones to which the particular identity of individuals should not matter). And since the legal historian is primarily concerned with change, and since (as these essays will emphasise) legal change is a very gradual business, confinement to the conventional periods would stifle inquiry.[11] Even if legal expertise were irrelevant, as Plucknett was so anxious to insist, the history of law could not usefully be treated as other kinds of history have come to be treated.

A related difference of approach is harder to formulate and does indeed have to do with legal expertise, but not in the obvious sense of knowing how lawsuits work and the like. The core business of the regular historian is the establishment of facts, one at a time: that of the lawyer is the analysis of situations, and therefore the consideration of many facts at the same time. The resulting difference in mental habit can most easily be illustrated by means of a caricature drawn from the experience of a law teacher. Students coming to the law from history too often assume that they can usefully read the books a page or even a chapter at a time. Those who come from mathematics or the natural sciences know that they must take it slowly, thinking each sentence through in relation to the last and then again in relation to the next.

It is this need to connect that nonlegal historians sometimes miss when dealing with legal history. The writer will hope to be forgiven for raking up an old irritation by way of example. What has been seen as his most heinous heresy was the proposition that the assize of novel disseisin did not begin as Maitland's protection of abstract possession but was originally aimed to protect tenants against arbitrary action by their lords.[12] Since one cannot see inside the mind of persons dead more than eight centuries, this rested essentially on a detailed correspondence between the words of the writ and things that we now know to have been happening. From nonlegal historians it attracted a fusillade of alternative explanations for each of the points of correspondence one by one, without regard for the cumulative improbability of the separate coincidences thereby postulated. One historian went further, objecting that if the writ was aimed against the plaintiff's lord it would surely have said so; and this overlooked the concomitant proposition about the sense of *disseise*. Seisin did not begin as an abstract concept of the same nature as possession: by definition a tenant could at first be seised and disseised only by his lord.[13]

Finally there is a more particular thought about the natural history of the legal historian. His work may be conditioned by the order in which he does it. Maitland's first big task was his edition of *Bracton's Note Book*; and to do it he mastered *Bracton* in a way that nobody had since the shadowy figures who worked on it in the thirteenth century (and nobody but S. E. Thorne has since). It has been suggested above that this influenced not just the immediate detail of "Pollock and Maitland" (*History of English Law*, 1895, 1898) but the lasting perception of the early common law as a system of the same nature as the developed Roman law. One can only wonder how differently the subject would have grown if Maitland's work had begun instead of ending with the editing of year books, which he saw as representing "a stage in the history of jurisprudence" earlier than anything in the surviving Roman evidence.

In the hope that it may be of some interest (and at the risk of a count of indecent exposure being added to the usual charge of heresy), the writer will plunge yet deeper into autobiography; and, for what it may be worth, a chronological list of his writings will be appended to this introduction. His own first big task was to get ready for publication an early legal text prepared by an editor who was neither lawyer nor historian but one of a small band of scholars drawn to the medieval common law by an interest in the Norman-French language.[14] *Novae Narrationes* is a formulary of the claims and denials to be made in the principal actions available in the thirteenth and fourteenth centuries; and what at the time seemed the serious need was to provide an introduction explaining the function of each of the actions, for most of which information was altogether lacking in secondary sources and hard to come by anywhere.[15] It was an interesting nightmare. But the legacy of that job in the writer's mind was a largely subconscious fretting about the properties of a legal world in which lawsuits consisted in claim and denial, oath and supernatural test. That was the world from which the year books grew, as it were the starting point of our law and perhaps of any law. And that fretting was no doubt the starting point of the various "natural history" ventures that have culminated in these essays.[16]

The writer's next big task, at the instance of the Cambridge University Press, was in some way to bring "Pollock and Maitland" up to date: an honor but another nightmare. An early decision was that tinkering with the text would be merely impious, and that conclusion increasingly seemed fortunate. You can rewrite sentences when you find reason to question particular propositions; but if it is not particular propositions you question but the way they are put together, you would have to rewrite the book. So the original text and introduction were reproduced unchanged and a new introduction was added, as it were an anticreed of disbeliefs. The personal actions gave no great trouble, because the writer (bothered by the meanings given to *trespass* and *covenant*) had already set out most of his heresies on these.[17] But even the modern land law had puzzled him,[18] and the history as given in "Pollock and Maitland," and therefore in all later books, was just a source of discontent that resisted formulation. Unreliable memory suggests that the alternative vision just came, almost (but not quite) all of a piece.[19] But there is a single particular recollection: a sudden idea about the sense of *seisin* and *disseisin* came one evening while waiting at Charing Cross station for a train home. In retrospect that seems to have been the starting point.

Debts to friends are never quantifiable. Mr. Derek Hall's edition had drawn fresh attention to *Glanvill*; and it is hard to think that Maitland could have written as he did if he had immersed himself in *Glanvill* half as fully as he had in *Bracton*. Oversights may have been easy because *Glanvill*'s most revealing statements come not in a focused discussion but in almost throwaway lines peripheral to the book's stated purpose.[20] Any historian can too easily forget that his sources were addressed not to him but to people who shared their writers' concerns and assumptions. The extent of another debt is something that even today the writer cannot estimate. Professor Thorne's lecture on inheritance was first given in Cambridge;[21] but the writer heard only a second reading in Oxford, where the presiding medievalist brought the occasion to its close by saying they would look forward to the footnotes. The lecture, delivered at machine-gun speed, is hard to follow even in the tranquillity of print; and at the time probably nobody, including Thorne and the writer, realized that it had fallen into the gulf of incomprehension between law and history. Thorne was apparently taken by historians to assert as a fact that regular inheritance came later than they had thought, and no footnotes could support that as a statement about what actually happened in the twelfth century. But his real proposition was not about who succeeded but about how undoubted successions were perceived. Each tenant held only for life, and when he died his lord was obliged to accept the heir for another life; and regular fulfillment of this obligation to create successive life tenancies came to be seen as the automatic devolution of an "ownership." Each heir was now understood to take not by fresh grant from his lord but by operation of an impersonal law. For what it is worth, the writer now believes that this shift, the unforeseeable end product of legislation in 1176, was even slower than Thorne supposed and the final perception of inheritance (and therefore of ownership) correspondingly later.[22]

The writer's own recollection of that afternoon in Oxford,[23] and incredulous remarks made later by historian friends in Yale,[24] attest Thorne's own belief in the importance of that lecture; and just recently one of his Harvard students has in conversation recalled a puzzled ruefulness at the way it had been received (or ignored). From the bibliography accompanying the new introduction to Pollock and Maitland it appears that in 1968 the writer had not absorbed either the precise significance of the lecture or the precise way it had been misunderstood.[25] But of course he saw its relevance. By chance (on his way to a visit in Yale) he stayed with Thorne in Harvard while that introduction was in the press, anxiously expressed the hope that Thorne himself still believed in the lecture, and was perplexed at the guarded response: "Nobody can produce charters or anything to show it is wrong." The introduction itself was not discussed, and an approving letter Thorne wrote when it reached him came as a huge relief. But (to put the matter in the most basic terms) there is no telling whether the writer could have conceived his heresy, first centered on novel disseisin, without Thorne's insight into mort d'ancestor.

The difficulty of exposition that comes with heresy was brought home to the writer when he then produced an elementary book.[26] His own understanding was so different from that of Maitland (and therefore of everybody else) that an attempt to place his account within the traditional framework seemed doomed to unintelligibility, so he simply started afresh; but the unease thereby provoked drove him in a second edition to attempt some parallel statement (though it was still uneasy). At both the pedagogic and the scholarly levels the difficulty is the same: discussion cannot be satisfactory when the parties start from different premises, and the writer was addressing readers devoutly faithful to Maitland's premises.

The writer had still not quite learned this lesson when he attempted detailed and documented exposition in Maitland Memorial lectures given in Cambridge in 1972 and published four years later.[27] Reflection now suggests a serious twist to what has been just an amusing memory: perhaps he would have made the printed version clearer if he could have seen the faces of the lecture audience. Rota power cuts switched the lights off punctually at the beginning of each lecture and on again at the end, and the candles kindly provided for him reached only his notes. Even for the blackboard (and the property law of any period is best explained by drawing horizontal and vertical lines) he had to point with a torch, and he could hardly keep shining that around a senior and distinguished gathering. So he lacked the facial feedback with which student audiences have always unwittingly signaled both comprehension and incomprehension—and to the lecturer alone in the dark it all seemed so clear.

It still does of course. The evidence of *Glanvill* about what lords' courts could properly do without writ, and the evidence of early plea rolls about what they actually did, are both beyond argument.[28] Neither was mentioned by Maitland, or probably even known to him. But for many historians his authority still entrenches his vision of novel disseisin as a possessory remedy, as it were protection against casual thieves of land; and the natural conclusion from the evidence is considered (or rather not considered) as unthinkable heresy. Or take the idea of "writs of right" as being about ownership: the lecturer in the dark innocently imagined he was putting paid to that as he pointed his torch at those horizontal and vertical lines on the blackboard.[29] Two decades later he was driven to seize the opportunity of a conference paper to make another attempt, counting plea roll entries to show that in getting on for half of all early writs of right the question was "vertical": whether the one party was entitled to hold the disputed land of the other or that other to have it free of the tenancy.[30] That can have nothing to do with Maitland's nineteenth-century vision of landownership, especially as defined in terms of longer possession. But for most historians Maitland's vision remains, as immune to statistics as it had been to lines on a blackboard. The sun and stars still go dutifully round the earth. And his earth is still flat: there can be no "vertical" disputes about ownership and possession.

We come back to that gulf between lawyers and historians. The writer's essential concern has always been with the reconstruction of legal thinking rather than the historians' establishment of facts. But his legal analysis obviously carries implications for the facts of social and economic history. At the earthiest level the "possessory" view of novel disseisin and mort d'ancestor, both extremely common in the plea rolls, conjures up an almost comic-strip society in which goodies were constantly assailed by baddies—by mere thieves of land and by prospectors for funerals. And the land caught up in all this agitation was neither empty waste nor the houses and gardens of modern suburbia, things that in principle could indeed be taken without consequence to anyone but taker and victim. As the means of production and livelihood it was both the heart of the economy and also the center of a network of obligations in which a mere taking was as unthinkable as the theft of a "tied cottage" (or of the job itself) would be today.[31]

The chronological list of writings that follows this introduction suggests a final thought. The earliest articles dealt with the personal actions and sprang from a long-standing unhappiness about the meanings given to *trespass* and *covenant*. An idea about trespass in particular seemed obvious. But, as the last of these essays will explain, only scraps of direct evidence for the "new" meaning could be found: it just made sense of everything that happened. That unhappiness dated back to undergraduate days, and if there was a specific trigger it is beyond recall.[32] But triggers can be identified for each of the other principal inquiries the writer has pursued. The "natural history" line of thought unquestionably sprang from *Novae Narrationes*; and that was not a job the writer chose or ever would have chosen. He was in effect coerced by Mr. Howard Drake, the persuasive secretary who kept the Selden Society going through the decline of its then literary director. The "feudalism" line of thought sprang from the Cambridge Press's commission to do something about "Pollock and Maitland"; and of course the only coercion was that of an honor it was unthinkable to refuse. But, though by that time he had come to terms with the modern land law, it is unlikely that the writer would ever of his own will have turned to what seemed its hopelessly elusive history. Perhaps the moral is that you choose projects on the basis of the received learning, which you hope to elaborate: it is the tasks you are set that may lead you to question that basis.

1. "Not Doing is No Trespass; A View of the Boundaries of Case", [1954] *Cambridge Law Journal* 105; *Studies* (no.19 below) 91

2. "Formedon before *De Donis*," 72 *Law Quarterly Review* (1956) 391; *Studies* 223 (noting a find made casually while searching plea rolls for personal actions)

3. "Trespass from Henry III to Edward III," 74 *Law Quarterly Review* (1958) 195, 407, 561; *Studies* 1

4. "Richard Hunne's *Praemunire*," 76 *English Historical Review* (1961) 80; *Studies* 145 (like 2 above noting a casual find)

5. "Sale of Goods in the Fifteenth Century'," 77 *Law Quarterly Review* (1961) 257; *Studies* 105

6. *Novae Narrationes* (Legal Introduction), 80 Selden Society (1963)

7. "Reason in the Development of the Common Law' (inaugural lecture at LSE)," 81 *Law Quarterly Review* (1965) 496; *Studies* 149.

8. "Theodore Frank Thomas Plucknett, 1897–1965," 51 *Proceedings of the British Academy* (1965) 505; *Studies* 279.

9. "Account Stated in the Action of Debt," 82 *Law Quarterly Review* (1966) 534; *Studies* 133.

10. "Law and Fact in Legal Development," 17 *University of Toronto Law Journal* (1967) 1; *Studies* 171.

11. *Pollock and Maitland's History of English Law* (introduction and bibliography to reissue of 1968; Cambridge University Press).

12. *Historical Foundations of the Common Law* (London, 1969, 2d ed. 1981).

13. Review of Grant Gilmore's *The Death of Contract*, 84 *Yale Law Journal* (1975) 1585; *Studies* 191.

14. *The Legal Framework of English Feudalism* (Cambridge, 1976).

15. "The Nature of Blackstone's Achievement," *Selden Society Lecture Series* (1980), and 1 *Oxford Journal of Legal Studies* (1981) 1; *Studies* 197.

16. "F. W. Maitland" (British Academy Lecture on a Master-Mind), 66 *Proceedings of the British Academy* (for 1980) 265; *Studies* 261.

17. "The Past and the Future of Judge-Made Law" (Wilfred Fullagar Memorial Lecture), 8 *Monash University Law Review* (1981) 1; *Studies* 209.

18. "Inheritance by Women in the Twelfth and Early Thirteenth Centuries," in *On the Laws and Customs of England: Essays in Honor of Samuel E. Thorne,* ed. M. S. Arnold, T. A. Green, S. A. Scully, S. D. White (Chapel Hill, 1981) 60; *Studies* 231.

19. *Studies in the History of the Common Law* (London and Ronceverte, 1985), reprinting nos. 1–5, 7–10, 13, 15–18. The volume of course has its own pagination, but pagination in the

originals is noted at the bottom of each page. A concordance to the originals is printed below.

20. *Sources of English Legal History*, jointly with J. H. Baker (London, 1986; Professor Baker contributed by far the larger share).

21. "The Origin of Prerogative Wardship," in *Law and Government in Medieval England and Normandy: Essays in Honour of Sir James Holt*, ed. G. Garnett and J. Hudson (Cambridge, 1994) 223.

22. "Maitland and the Grand Assize," 7 *Haskins Society Journal* for 1995 (Woodbridge and Rochester, N.Y., 1997) 151.

23. " 'Pollock and Maitland': A Lawyer's Retrospect" in *The History of English Law: Centenary Essays on "Pollock and Maitland,"* ed. J. Hudson, 89 *Proceedings of the British Academy* (Oxford, 1996) 243.

24. "Samuel Edmund Thorne, 1907–1994," 142 *Proceedings of the American Philosophical Society* (1998) 161.

25. "Maitland" (address at the unveiling of a memorial tablet to F. W. Maitland in Westminster Abbey) [2001] *Cambridge Law Journal* 265.

26. "What Was a Right of Entry?" [2002] *Cambridge Law Journal* 561.

In this book references to most of the articles above are to their reprinted form in *Studies*, no. 19. For any readers who may wish to look them up, but have easier access to the originals than to the volume of reprints, there follows a concordance:

pp. 1–90 reprint no. 3
pp. 91–103 reprint no. 1
pp. 105–32 reprint no. 5
pp. 133–44 reprint no. 9

pp. 145–47 reprint no. 4
pp. 149–70 reprint no. 7
pp. 171–89 reprint no. 10
pp. 191–96 reprint no. 13
pp. 197–208 reprint no. 15
pp. 209–22 reprint no. 17
pp. 223–29 reprint no. 2
pp. 231–60 reprint no. 18
pp. 261–77 reprint no. 16
pp. 279–93 reprint no. 8

A NATURAL HISTORY OF THE COMMON LAW

I
MAKING LAW:
LAWYERS AND LAYMEN

THERE IS A REASON FOR BEGINNING THIS ESSAY with a question it will not discuss, namely the influence of Roman law upon English law. This has been a perennial topic among English legal historians, partly because in England (as elsewhere in Europe) the study of Roman law was being revived in the twelfth and early thirteenth centuries, the very time from which hard English evidence begins. There has been a strong sense that there *ought* to have been an influence, and this has provoked disappointment in some historians and a rummage for examples (of varying plausibility) in others. This essay will suggest that there could not be much effect beyond whatever intangible force may have been exerted by language. Our early sources are in Latin and inevitably use words which for Roman lawyers were technical terms. Historians have been tempted to read those words in the English sources with their Roman connotations, and there is a real question (especially in the area of property) how far English lawyers at the time had those connotations in mind. But that is very different from the more direct kind of influence historians have sought, namely the borrowing of Roman answers for English questions. The most elegant of answers is no use until the question has been asked; and the point of this essay is that early lawsuits settle disputes without raising questions of substantive law and that progress depends upon procedural changes which allow such questions to emerge.[1]

The thirteenth-century *Bracton*, which sought to give a comprehensive account of English law, has a sophisticated discussion of the liability of borrowers. Whereas a loan of money passes property in the actual coins to the borrower, the loan of a specific object does not; and (since in general risk is understood to go with property) it follows that while the borrower of money contracts an incorporeal obligation which cannot be affected by any mishap to the particular coins handed over, the borrower of a specific object may escape liability if it is lost or destroyed without his fault.[2] Nothing could be clearer, but only in a legal system which has articulated ideas of property in chattels and of fault, and the analysis in *Bracton* came not from English experience but from Roman books.

In English courts at that time nothing could happen to make a difference between the two kinds of loan.[3] The lender of money or object complained in set terms that the borrower was withholding it, the borrower made a set denial of liability, and the case was settled by the testing of oaths, by compurgation. The borrower swore that he was not liable, and neighbors swore to him; and if they all got their lines right, the borrower had won. Or rather (and the correction goes to the heart of this essay) the "alleged borrower" had won. His unvarying oath went to present liability, not to past particular facts; and nobody but he knew whether its basis was that he had never borrowed, or had repaid the money or returned the object, or could not do so because of an accidental loss, or had been told by the plaintiff that he need not do so, or anything else one might think of as relevant. If questions like accidental loss were raised at all, it might be in discussion between defendant and those he was trying to recruit as oath helpers, or perhaps between defendant and priest: would his soul be in peril if he swore his oath? But they were not questions for law courts.

Now back to that passage in *Bracton*: if it could not relate to anything in the English lawsuit, why was it included in a book on "The Laws and Customs of England"? One of the characteristics of law seen as a system of substantive rules is that the rules can be discussed as entities in themselves without reference to what actually happens in court. Law teachers in England do it all the time, not always to the benefit of their students. It was in those terms that his Roman learning had taught the *Bracton* writer to think. He may have known that his second-hand propositions about the borrower's liability did not apply in England and just thought they ought to. Or he may have supposed that they applied within the defendant's oath, so that though English lawsuits did not articulate them they still yielded the "right" answers. Or he may just have been locked inside his abstractions and not tried to connect them with what actually happened in court. But I am sure he understood them.

They would be understood by all readers sharing the ecclesiastical, literate, Latinate background of the *Bracton* writer, the civil service which long provided the clerical staff of the royal courts and at first also much of the judiciary. It was such men that brought about this transient contact between two legal systems more than a millennium apart in development. But though they continued to be clerks in the Chancery and in the courts, so that writs and plea rolls continued to be in Latin, they were slowly excluded from the bench. Royal judges ceased altogether to be

recruited from church and university and came to be chosen only
from those who practiced in English courts. For relevant reasons
to which we shall come, the English lawsuit was becoming a
more complex affair than arranging tests for blank oaths, and it
was the practitioner's skill that the judge now needed. His working language was no longer Latin, in which he was not at home,
and he was not learned in Roman law and would soon give up
struggling with Bracton. But in the later thirteenth century efforts
were made to keep him in touch with the Latinate world. The
formal claims and denials made in court, for example, were always in French, writs always in Latin. But somebody thought it
useful to produce a combined formulary for the new men, so just
for this once the writs are given in French.[4]

Near the end of the thirteenth century some optimist even
tried to make Bracton itself user-friendly, producing a much
abridged version in French. It correctly translates the passage
about the liability of borrowers, then ventures a comment of its
own: a debtor is to blame if he shows a lot of money in public,
and it is his fault if it is stolen from him.[5] This man at least has
got the Latin sense but missed the Roman point, which was that
fault was irrelevant where money or other fungibles were concerned. And for him it was probably still the case, as it was when
the Bracton passage was written, that the question was not related to anything in his experience because it would not arise for discussion in court. But that was soon to change. As the thirteenth
century turned to the fourteenth, plea rolls and year books show
a few cases in which instead of the general denial a bailee actually explains in court that he cannot return the thing because it was
stolen or the like.[6] What was happening? Had the Roman mes-
sage, as transmitted through Bracton, got through? That was indeed to happen, but in the eighteenth century rather than the thirteenth; and even then it would be repeated but not heeded.[7]

What got through to English lawyers toward the end of the thirteenth century was not Roman book learning but the actual facts behind some English lawsuits. About the time that French abridgment of *Bracton* was made, an early year book report shows lawyers in court struggling with a bailment. A document of title had been handed for safekeeping to a married woman, and after her husband's death she is sued for its return. The argument for her is that as a married woman at the time she could not bind herself in contract. The argument for the plaintiff is that she has got his property. These lawyers were not thinking about the Roman learning of *Bracton*: they were at the start of the life cycle, trying to analyze a bailment for the first time.[8]

The bailment story will not be taken further. What makes it interesting in the present context is that brief encounter with past Roman ideas. The encounter was fruitless because it happened in books. Those first stirrings of discussion were prompted not by books but by procedural changes which were making it possible for facts to emerge from within the general denial. If there is such a thing as a legal life cycle, its first stage is precisely the kind of lawsuit we have been considering: a set formula of claim or accusation is met by a set general denial, and the dispute is resolved by making one side or the other swear to his case and subjecting the oath to some supernatural test. Such litigation can generate very precise rules about procedure and penalties but no more substantive law than the commandments implicit in a formulary of claims and denials. It is when the dispute has to be decided by people instead of by putting a blank oath to supernatural test that questions are asked and have to be answered. That change is the second stage of our supposed life cycle, and in England it happened within the reach of evidence.

There was of course more to it than a single event. But a central part was played by a single change early in the thirteenth century in the treatment of accusations of serious wrong, and it was made more cataclysmic by an earlier change which must be described first. There had been three kinds of test. If the accuser was himself witness to the fact, he could in certain kinds of case swear an affirmative oath which would be tested by battle. If there was no specific witness, an accusation arising from the suspicion of neighbors (the ancestor of the grand jury) would put the accused to answer by swearing an oath of denial, and that oath would be tested in one of two ways depending on what we should call corroboration. If there was something like a corpse or a wound to back the accusation up, the test would be by ordeal: fire or water would certify the oath as true or false. But if there was no more than neighborhood suspicion, the accused's oath of denial would be tested by compurgation, by neighbors swearing to him. This last situation was changed by legislative act in the middle of the twelfth century: compurgation was excluded, and an accusation arising from even uncorroborated suspicion would now put a defendant to ordeal.[9] Except for appeals of felony, that is cases prosecuted by a victim who had seen the wrong and could prove it by battle, all serious wrongs now led to trial by ordeal.

To mount an ordeal you needed a priest to tell the fire or the water to distinguish the truthful innocent from the guilty liar. The validity of such commands had long been questioned; and if one can think of a single event as jolting the common law out of that ancient first stage of its life cycle, it was a ruling by the Roman Church, promptly obeyed in England, that priests were no longer to play that part.[10] The ban was specific to ordeals: priests were not to conjure elements like fire and water. The testing of oaths as such was not questioned: battle survived, though falling into disuse; and as for compurgation, the church courts themselves long thought it appropriate when there was only one man's word against another. But now that the Church had, as it were, withdrawn its labor, ordeals were finished.

In the field of what we should call serious crime this brought the legal process to an abrupt stop, and the lay power had to think of something else to do with accused persons piling up in its prisons. The ancient comfortable reliance on God to test an oath sworn by the defendant was at an end, and mortal men, with their own souls to worry about, would have to swear not just to his credibility but directly to his guilt or innocence. It must have been an upset beyond modern imagination.

There were precedents for allowing a defendant to choose to stake his case on the sworn verdict of men of the neighborhood instead of having his own oath put to a divine test. For one accused of serious crime, even by uncorroborated suspicion, there was now no divine test he could choose; but he still had to "choose" jury trial. His only alternative was to stay uncomfortably in prison, and the end of the factual story is that the discomfort became a literally crushing pressure to put himself on a verdict of the countryside.[11] But our concern is not that unpalatable story but legal development, and (if one can think in the large terms of human history) it is important to emphasise the chronology. We shall see that there had probably been a similar upset in Rome, but if so it happened long before surviving evidence. The Church decision which ended English ordeals was made in 1215, and that was twenty years after the earliest of our surviving plea rolls. The minutes of the common law, now preserved through eight centuries, begin in that ancient first stage.

The upset caused by the Church's decision can be seen as a reenactment in the legal arena of the Fall of Man. Telling good from evil, deciding between Guilty and Not Guilty, brought up questions even more painful than "Was this the man that did it?" Was he Guilty if yes he did it, but by accident or mistake or under duress or out of necessity or when sleepwalking or drunk or mad? A developed system of law is one in which the answers to such questions are written out in books from which the judge can, as it were, read extracts to the jury. But there was no book of answers in 1215 or for centuries to come: the questions had yet to be asked.

The writer is always in trouble with criminal lawyers for saying that the early history of their subject can be shortly told. There is little to say because all the questions which would interest us were asked and answered in the jury room, sealed within a general verdict as inscrutably as they had been in the outcome of an ordeal. Criminal trials were heard locally, the accused normally had no counsel, and almost never was a law reporter present to tell us even what was said openly in court, let alone privately among the jurors. And the plea roll would record only the general verdict: Guilty or Not Guilty. Comparisons of plea rolls with coroners' rolls have given glimpses of enlightenment,[12] but we are unlikely to learn much of the stages by which neighborhood ideas of justice became a uniform system of criminal law.

We can, however, be fairly sure of the mechanism. Criminal juries were not allowed the luxury of a special verdict, saying what had happened and leaving the court to declare the legal effect. But they could look to the judge for guidance on the significance of facts. What he told them came to be seen as prescriptive, an instruction derived from a known body of law. But it must have begun as an attempt to direct their minds, to focus their own standards and make their own decision. The responsible judge, if unsure what advice he should give, could arrange to have the case held over while the question was discussed among his fellows in London. Systematization came about as questions arising at the trial in the country were carried back for discussion in London, and juries directed in the light of that discussion. The central core

of the criminal law must have existed informally around the din-
ner tables of the Inns long before it emerged in judgments about
the correctness of a jury direction. But those traditions in the Inns
were not spun out of the heads of lawyers: the raw materials were
the ideas of ordinary laymen, and the finished product had to remain consonant with those ideas or be disregarded by juries.

So far as it was a common-law process therefore, the entire
development of the criminal law took place within the framework
of the general issue, in dialogue between lawyers and laymen
about what it was to be Guilty or Not Guilty. In civil cases development was more fragmented. We leave for a later essay the
development of property in land, where something quite different
was going on. But the area known today as the law of torts, and
to a lesser extent the law of contract, was similarly teased out in
centuries of litigation, though not by the single mechanism of the
jury direction.

In those areas nearly all early disputes were heard in local
courts, where they mostly ended in compurgation as in our case
of the loan. A defendant who believed in God and hell would not
swear lightly. Nor would he persuade neighbors to swear to him
if they were not sure of him, and the court might have some discretion in setting the number of neighbors he must produce. Beyond the religious pressure, the community pressure was great;
and the city of London, a mercantile community totally dependent on trust between its members, took steps to protect compurgation when jury trial threatened to encroach.[13] If swearing was
a serious matter, so was putting another to his oath; and this may
be why, though litigation in local courts was cheap, many disputes were not fought but settled. Perhaps they included cases of
legal doubt.

But our concern is not with the suppression of doubts but
their emergence into the open, and this came about as the blank

compurgation was replaced by jury trial, a process governed by jurisdictional accidents. In its early days the king's court sat locally, in principle dealing with one county at a time. In the local setting, there was nothing to raise disquiet about compurgation. When royal justice was centralized geographically, with cases coming to a single court sitting in Westminster, oath helpers would not be neighbors but strangers who came to be hired, and there was dissatisfaction. But compurgation remained in frequent use until the sixteenth century.

Another accident, however, confined it to what we should call contract and excluded it from tort. Contract cases came to qualify for royal as opposed to local justice effectively on the basis of the amount at stake. But actions for wrongs were for the jurisdiction whose law had been broken, and they could come to the king's court only if they were said to have been committed in breach of the king's special law, his peace. That had once been a serious wrong within the twelfth-century exclusion of compurgation. So tort actions, which went to the king's court only if breach of his peace was alleged, there carried jury trial from the beginning. When in the fourteenth century such actions were permitted to come to royal courts without mention of the king's peace, logic would have permitted those defendants to prove their denial by compurgation.[14] But logic was resisted, and all tort actions in royal courts went to jury trial.

One might expect therefore that enunciation of the law concerning civil wrongs would follow exactly the pattern of criminal wrongs, the whole law of torts being slowly made explicit in directions to juries. That would have happened if civil cases had been confined as rigidly as criminal cases to general issue and general verdict. But, unlike criminal defendants, civil litigants could have lawyers, and mechanical differences in the conduct of litigation gave the lawyers other opportunities for argumentation.[15]

A criminal case was heard throughout by a single court and in the presence of the jury in the country. There was no more precise formulation of the question than the invariable plea of Not Guilty. A civil case began and finished in Westminster: but it was not ordinarily practicable to get a jury there, so arrangements had to be made for the issue reached in Westminster to be put to a jury in the country by judges on circuit. The verdict would then be reported back to the court in Westminster, which would give judgment accordingly. In principle therefore there were three possible occasions for discussion: first in Westminster, then before the jury in the country (long the only formal opportunity in a criminal case), then back in Westminster when the verdict was reported. It was the first of these that first came into play. The civil defendant, unlike the criminal, might in exceptional circumstances be allowed to plead something other than the usual general issue, precisely because a fallible human jury might be misled by deceptive facts.

Take a real case.[16] An epileptic fit was understood to be possession by devils, which could be driven out by beating the sufferer. The sufferer sues, and the defendant fears what a jury will do if he pleads the usual Not Guilty. It was after all he who had got all that blood on the floor. So he confesses the fact of the battery and seeks to avoid liability by expressly making his justification of (in our terms) proper medical treatment. This of course is not a final answer as the general issue would be. The plaintiff must reply to the plea, and he has a choice. He can assert that the battery was committed not for the reason alleged but out of the defendant's wickedness, and a jury in the country will be asked not for a general verdict but to say whether the admitted battery was or was not for the reason alleged. No other question is left open and judgment will automatically follow the verdict. Alternatively the plaintiff may, but only if he admits that the defendant beat him for the reason alleged, argue that it was not a sufficient reason, that one is not justified in beating somebody just because he is possessed by devils. This is a demurrer; and, since all the facts are now admitted on both sides, there is no question to send to a jury in the country. There is only a question of substantive law for a dismayed bench of judges to decide (or not).

The expertise involved in making and answering special pleas instead of going to the general issue transformed the learning of pleaders and was largely responsible for early reporting in the year books. This was also why the king's judges came to be appointed from among practicing pleaders rather than from the Latinate civil service; and it is ironic that the kind of man who thought in terms of substantive law was pushed aside by the very process which was raising questions in those terms for the first time in English lay courts. To some of the questions clerical judges would have had ready-made Roman answers. The new men had to think out their own, and evidently did not like being asked the questions. Often no judgment was recorded even when the parties had staked the case on the point of law. And since they could do that only at the cost of admitting all the facts, the common thing in the year books is that the point is raised for discussion, but in the end the case goes off on a point of fact or even on the general issue. What the year book reader then got was only an indication: in this case counsel did not dare risk staking his client's case on the legal question.

So in itself the replacement of compurgation by jury trial had not done much to generate an explicit law of torts. If one tries to imagine a Prosser or a Winfield early in the sixteenth century sitting down with all the year books on his table to write a textbook, the product would have been scrappy: as it were a lot of blank pages with scattered single assertions about things like beating epileptics and pulling down houses to halt the spread of fires. But such an enterprise would not have entered anybody's head. The nearest you could sensibly get would be a book arranged by kinds of action, under each of which would be set out cases showing what pleas had and had not been found acceptable. But since the logic which made a special plea acceptable might apply in various kinds of action, the best thing you could do with the year books was to abridge them, arranging in alphabetical order all the topics on which you could foresee a pleader seeking guidance, and under each heading putting abstracts of relevant cases in essentially random order. A computer would have been ideal.

But all this was concerned only with things that could be pleaded specially. The logic was fear that a jury of laymen would be confused by the general issue. They might know that the defendant had done the deed, but not know or not give proper effect to the facts which he thought justified it. What mattered was deceptiveness, not difficulty. A jury might find it difficult to decide between Guilty and Not Guilty if the harm had been accidental. But that was their problem, as it was in a criminal trial, and there was no special plea of accident. Most of classical tort law still remained in hiding.

It was further procedural changes between the fifteenth century and the seventeenth that were to generate enough legal statement to make a book. Even then the process was slow. Textbooks on tort law did not appear until the middle of the nineteenth century, the earliest on the western shore of the Atlantic. The essence of these changes, much less coherent than a summary will suggest, is that the first stage of a lawsuit, pleading to reach an issue to be sent to a jury in the country, ceased to be done orally in court and came instead to be done by exchanging papers. It was no longer possible to fly kites. On the face of it you now had to make your plea or not, and the other side had to take the point of law or not. But this seeming inflexibility was more than compensated for by new possibilities of discussion at the third stage of the lawsuit, when the verdict was reported back to the court in Westminster. Previously you could question the legal validity of a special plea only if you admitted the facts. The supposedly epileptic plaintiff had been compelled to choose whether to contest the lawfulness of beating him to drive out devils or to deny that this was in fact the defendant's motive for beating him. Under the new dispensation he could first deny that this had been the motive for the beating; but then, if the jury went against him on that, he could raise the point of law when the verdict was reported back to the court in Westminster. It did not matter that the defendant's motive had been found to be good, because the act was still unlawful. Points of law could be raised without risk, and answers would be declared formally in judgments rather than just indicated by lawyers abandoning pleas.

But the law so declared was still confined to matters which could be pleaded specially, and pleas in justification are not central to the law of torts. What is more, this was law made entirely by judges. It was indeed jury trial that had raised the question: these were facts which must not be left within the general issue because a jury might be misled. But jurors played no part in shaping the rule that the plea established.

A more important procedural change cut deeper, enabling questions which had previously been sealed up within the general issue to be discussed openly in court. The process was more complex than in criminal cases. First in civil cases, unlike criminal, it had always been possible to take a special verdict, and their widespread use would have been a prime means of compelling legal statement. At the end of the thirteenth century judges may have seen that and taken fright. In an action brought in 1290 by the owner of property destroyed in a catastrophic fire, the defense told a story of accident which was repeated in a special verdict. The jury even made an assessment of damages, in case the court decided there was liability. But there the record ends, and perhaps judgment was never given.[17] Except in certain kinds of property action,[18] special verdicts remained rare until the sixteenth century when, as will appear in a later essay, they were used to compel legal statement in situations in which uncertainty had become scandalous.[19]

More fruitful was a means of getting hold of facts hitherto sealed up in general verdicts. As in criminal cases, the handle was the direction to the jury, and as in criminal cases, it may be that the first mechanism was to have the point discussed before any direction was given. But since in civil cases the judge presiding at the trial acted not on his own authority but as a delegate of the court in Westminster, the stage at which the verdict was reported back offered a chance to argue that a direction actually given had been wrong. If the court in Westminster agreed, it would order a new trial before a fresh jury in the country; though various expedients, such as taking alternative verdicts on alternative directions, were devised to avoid the expense of starting over again.

It was this last process that brought up for decision most of the questions at the heart of nineteenth century tort law, particularly those concerning fault. In the case of some wrongs, such as battery, the formalities of the action had given no indication of the relevance of fault or accident; and as with criminal cases it was only when directions to juries could be questioned that the matter was discussed by lawyers.[20] Even in wrongs in which the plaintiff alleged fault, standards were hidden behind a plea of Not Guilty. The "reasonable man" who became so prominent in tort law started as a criterion by which judges sought to help jurors focus their own standards.

The development of tort law was therefore dominated by jury trial, to which in the kings's courts there was never any alternative. The first phase generated what modern lawyers would regard as the more peripheral rules, especially those concerning justifications. These arose from the need to permit departure from the general issue in deceptive situations for fear that jurors would go wrong. But juries had no input into those rules. The later phase, bringing out the core questions, was systematization of what jurors did with the general issue when it was left to them. Lay perceptions of right and wrong were articulated into rules of law.

The development of contract law, in contrast, was stifled by the continuing availability of compurgation. But, although available, it was never required. A defendant who could swear with casually recruited oath helpers could always choose a jury instead. This possibility generated some law for reasons akin to the confession and avoidance in tort, and the appearance around 1300 of special pleas of accidental loss by bailees, noted earlier in this essay,[21] is an example.

But most questions were still suppressed. The borrower of money who had repaid it obviously did not now owe, and he should take the general issue and go to compurgation or jury as he chose. Suppose he had borrowed in one county and repaid in another. If he chose a jury on the general issue, the jurors would come from the county of the loan and might not know of the repayment. So he argues that the county boundary makes the case deceptive, and seeks to confess the loan and make a special plea of the repayment so as to get a jury from the second county. But this is refused: he does not have to choose jury trial, and, since his own knowledge and conscience are not limited by geography, he can take the general issue and go to compurgation.[22]

It follows that all kinds of question obvious to us about part payment, forgiveness, and the like are not asked in a way that will generate formal answers. In the sixteenth century a defendant who had elected for compurgation explained before doing his swearing that his creditor had accepted payment of part of the debt and forgiven the residue now claimed, and he was told that on those facts he could not swear safely in conscience.[23] Perhaps it was not uncommon for such matters to come up in a process which has left few traces: one about to swear by compurgation underwent some process of examination and admonition, and it is conceivable that this dialogue between lawyers (or court clerks) and laymen played a part not unlike that of the direction to a jury. But such admonitions do not often feature in the reports, presumably because they were not seen as important for lawyers.[24] And, in ways to appear later, compurgation itself had essentially gone out of use by the time jury directions themselves could be questioned and considered in judgments. It was never more than a blank end to a lawsuit.

The availability of compurgation inevitably provoked efforts by plaintiffs to exclude it. It was argued for example that if the transaction had been made before witnesses the dispute should go to a jury of the countryside. But this argument failed on the simple ground that the general issue was normally a denial of present liability, not of past facts. A loan of money might have been publicly made, so that a jury would surely know of it. But the defendant would be denying not that he had borrowed the money but that he now owed it; and he did not owe if he had repaid, which he might have done in private.[25]

Nor could the lender feel safe even if he was confident of the honesty as well as the solvency of his borrower. The borrower might die, and the logic of compurgation had been pushed to a perverse conclusion. The defendant could swear only to what he himself knew. The borrower's executors could not know whether he had borrowed, still less whether he had repaid; and, because compurgation was not open to them, it was held that they could not be sued.[26] The prudent lender of a significant amount must therefore do more to guard himself than make his loan in front of witnesses. There were various devices, the simplest being to take a bond, a deed under seal in which the borrower confessed not the fact of his borrowing but that he was now indebted. The borrower could not then get to the general issue, that he did not owe. All he could do was to deny that this was his deed. That issue would go to a jury, which would compare seals and the like; but he would not deny his deed lightly, because if it was found to be his he was imprisoned for denying it.

This last feature reflects the importance of bonds in economic life,[27] and that in turn led to another difficulty. Suppose that the borrower had given a bond and had later paid, but had done so without procuring either the return of his bond or an acquittance under the lender's seal. There was nothing to stop the lender suing and recovering the money again. If the borrower could have taken the general issue to a jury, they would of course have said he did not owe: but he could not plead that he did not owe, because the plaintiff had his acknowledgment that he did. So far as the regular common law courts were concerned, that was the end of the matter. And here an altogether different mechanism of development came into play. The defendant turned to the equitable jurisdiction of the chancellor, who after long hesitation accepted that the unconscionable behavior of the lender in seeking to enforce the paid bond should outweigh the general interest in retaining the conclusive character of bonds; and on these facts he was prepared to grant an injunction requiring the lender to discontinue his action in the common-law court.

So far as the story of contract has yet been taken, a tiny part in its development was played by jury trial. The following essay will turn to the mechanisms by which ordinary contractual disputes were withdrawn from compurgation and put to juries and will suggest that the division between court and jury was again central to what happened. But whereas in tort the fruitful process was a kind of dialogue between the two, with judges articulating inchoate lay ideas of right and wrong, the contractual revolution seems at least in part to have been initiated by an absence of communication. Juries did what they saw as justice on the facts before them without caring (and probably without knowing) that their justice could not be squared with the legal proprieties. And judges, shut out from the jury's thought processes, could only accept a blank result, and in the end they were happy to do so. But that is for the following essay.[28]

The largest theme of this essay is that the generation of a system of substantive rules was a function of jury trial, or rather of the emergence of questions when inscrutable modes of decision were replaced by human deciders. A second theme is the fragmentary way in which this happened in the common law. The most unitary was crime in which all common-law development took place within the direction to the jury. This was true also of the central area of torts, though procedural differences produced explicit results in judgments earlier than in crime. And, earlier still, the process of special pleading, driven by fear and mistrust of human deciders, had generated discussion of peripheral matters. It seems perverse that defenses of necessity should have emerged earlier than rules about accident, and even more perverse that historians should long have deduced that accident was simply irrelevant.[29] But, to the reasonable observer from Mars or Rome (or even from schoolboy lessons in chemistry), nothing could seem so perverse as a debtor being sued for a debt he had paid and having to go to another court altogether to stop the action against him.

The common law has proved immensely strong. It crossed the Atlantic and reached the antipodes, and it has flourished in all its homes. But it came to those homes among the cultural baggage of emigrants. No society has reached out to choose it, as Roman law has been chosen. That fragmentation may have been responsible. Who would choose a system in which, to take the worst case, one might be driven to litigate in two separate courts, the one somehow working against the other? Perhaps ironically, the principal thing that other systems have chosen to borrow is the trust, a product of that jurisdictional opposition which would have been hard to conceive in a tidier environment. But untidiness is not attractive, and the English fragmentation is in stark contrast with the coherence of the Roman mechanism and consequently of the Roman law.

For most of the first life of Roman law, lawsuits were divided into two stages. There was a hearing before a magistrate, who then remitted the case for decision to a *judex*. But the judex was not a lawyer: in time indeed he came to consult lawyers. Nor, although drawn from a list of qualified persons, was he even an official. He was just a solid citizen, perhaps more nearly comparable with the knights of the county required for an English grand assize than with the lawful men of the neighborhood of an ordinary jury. At any rate he was a layman to whom the magistrate referred the case. But the reference was total and final: the judex did not report back to the magistrate but himself gave judgment. If the judex replaced some divine test of an oath, it happened so early as to be beyond the reach of evidence: but the division into two stages together with the prominence of oaths in the earliest general kind of action makes that likely.[30] At first the only change was that from irrational to rational. The old forms continued, and what the judex got was a package question like our general issue, to which he gave an equally package answer.

When important changes came, it was at the first stage of the lawsuit: discussion before the magistrate produced a result like that of pleading, and this was crystallized in a formula of instruction by which the magistrate referred the case to the judex. But whereas English special pleading broke the dispute up, extracting one single point on which the parties agreed to stake the case, the Roman formula had to convey a single instruction which would leave every aspect of the case to the judex: if you find this and that but not the other, give judgment for the plaintiff (either for a fixed amount or for as much as seemed proper). Essentially the magistrate in that one document could be playing the equivalent of many English parts: that of the administrative Chancery in granting a new writ, that of the equitable Chancery in allowing a new equitable remedy or defense, and up to a point that of the judge in directing a jury (though this is partly reflected in the judex consulting a jurist). Nor is the coherence just that required by a single document: the formula is a single sentence, though sometimes with several conditional clauses. And the "if this, then that" form is legal statement as direct as that of the legislator. The single mechanism produced coherent law.

So in both systems the fruitful process was the instruction given to laymen by judge or magistrate, and discussion among Roman jurists and English barristers and judges about what that instruction should be. In England those discussions begin to emerge into the open in the seventeenth century; and in the eighteenth it was possible, for the first time since the romanesque attempt of *Bracton* five hundred years before, for Blackstone to give a coherent account of English law in more or less substantive terms.

That account began as lectures, and even at that time Blackstone would not have spoken in those terms if he had been addressing lawyers. Had he been lecturing in the Inns of Court, a practice obsolete by his day, what he said would have been all about procedure and incomprehensible to laymen. But he was lecturing in Oxford, and English law was not yet a university subject. His listeners were not law students but young gentlemen who would inherit seats in the House of Lords or buy them in the House of Commons or would be justices of the peace or at the very least county folk taking part in the public life of their communities. He was a lawyer seeking to explain to laymen a system of law which reached reasonable results behind institutions and procedures of quite unreasonable artificiality. It is possible that he had a Roman counterpart. The introduction to these essays suggested that English law seemed to reach in the eighteenth century a stage reached by Roman law in the second, and the comparison was between the writings of our solid Blackstone and those of the shadowy Gaius, about whom the only important fact we know is that he was a teacher.[31]

It turned out, of course, that for lawyers Blackstone was giving the game away. His exposure of the artificialities so horrified one of his listeners, the young Bentham, that Blackstone can be said to have inspired not only the textbooks of the nineteenth century but also that century's drive for legislative reform of the law. But, for the purpose of this essay, the important thing his lay audience had drawn from lawyer Blackstone was the vision of a system of substantive rules. In the common-law world this was a new discipline which reached its zenith in those confident years late in the nineteenth century when lawyers could write textbooks and think about the codification of particular areas of the law. But it is systems derived from the Roman that have gone in for comprehensive codes: the common law was still too untidy.

There is a postscript. In the Roman system the procedural division was abandoned as burdensome: why struggle to hammer out a precise and complex formula telling a judex what to do when the magistrate could decide the case himself? Those who know about Roman law say that decline followed, principle being lost in detail. In England we have done the equivalent in civil cases by effectively abolishing the civil jury, and with the same result. Judges now find the facts for themselves and set them out in their judgments, and the law is enmeshed in detail to an extent unthinkable when it had to be encapsulated in a jury direction. Whatever the administrative saving, the law itself is changing in texture without the discipline of concise statement which had to be both intelligible and acceptable to laymen. But juries remain in crime; and in tort acceptability to a sense of personal justice may not matter so much if, as seems to be the case, tort law is moving away from a basis in personal responsibility and toward reallocation of risks on policy grounds.[32]

II

CHANGING LAW:
FICTIONS AND FORMS

THE PREVIOUS ESSAY WAS CONCERNED WITH the ways in which substantive law (other than property law) comes into being. This one turns to the means by which it changes. A court guided by its own customs had no difficulty in accommodating to new conditions, and if an adjustment seemed desirable it might expressly announce what it proposed to do in the future.[1] One of my teachers remembered what he thought an absurd notice pinned up in his school: "As from next term it will be a custom of the school that." But it is not absurd. And in a custom-based court it is not only possible but likely that such an announcement would be part of the decision of a case which had exposed an awkwardness in the existing customary arrangements.[2] Legislation is not something separate, and of course it will have no greater binding force than the custom amended. And some of this attitude carried over into the king's courts, which at first treated legislative acts as internal amendments to a body of custom in their keeping rather than as commands from outside and above.[3]

But the kind of change you can make depends upon the kind of custom or rule to which you work. You cannot have substantive legislation until you are applying substantive rules. It is in property law, which always had a large substantive content, that major changes were made by legislation from the early days of the common law, though when we turn to property in the following essays we shall see that the changes that ensued often went far beyond what was intended. In the area of obligations, however, a main point of the preceding essay was that the emergence of substantive rules was very slow. Textbooks did not appear until the middle of the nineteenth century, and naturally there was no substantive legislation. Apart from adjustments over jurisdiction and process, the only statute until modern times to play much of a part with contract or tort was the Statute of Frauds late in the seventeenth century, and that was concerned with proof.[4] So how did change come about? Obviously it came about (or at least came to be formalized) in litigation; and one has only to look at reports and pleadings down to the nineteenth century to see that an important part must have been played by fiction. And a principal aim of this essay is to try to work out what that part was, to discern the truth behind the fictions. Who was doing what, and why?

Sir Henry Maine identified fiction as one of the means by which law was kept in touch with changing needs, the others being equity and legislation;[5] and the last two are both means of purposeful change, though in different degree. Was fiction as purposeful as it may look to unthinking hindsight? Bentham's indignation fortified his usual certainty: fiction was a "wilful falsehood, having for its object the stealing of legislative power, by and for hands which could not . . . openly claim it, and, but for the delusion thus produced, could not exercise it."[6] But it cannot make sense to imagine lawyers leaping from their baths with a sordid Eureka: "Here is a pack of lies that should do the trick." And what sort of lawyers would they be? For Bentham the thieving hands were those of judges consciously stealing legislative power. But only conspiracy theory on a sublime scale could see judges as responsible for fictions, colluding at least with plaintiffs' lawyers. This essay will suggest that the part of judges in fictional change was essentially passive. They might facilitate the later stages of a fictional development, but in the important early stages they just accepted results reached by others.

It is only with legislation and conveyancing, and up to a point with equity, that one can think of a controlling mind identifying deficiencies in the law and devising remedies. The minds behind other change were those of countless individual lawyers through the centuries, each concerned not with "the law" as such but with a small immediate predicament of his client. Nor were lawyers alone responsible for the changes that came about. We shall find reason to think that an important part was played by jurors, not in the kind of constructive dialogue with judges envisaged in the preceding essay but in lack of communication between the two. Jurors were shut up by themselves, returning blank verdicts and making unexplained awards of damages; and this enabled them to do their own justice, not caring (and perhaps not knowing) that their justice was not strictly according to the judges' law.

There are of course "deliberate" fictions, most obviously the device by which legislator or conveyancer may use an "as if" clause as shorthand to import a known package of desired consequences. Before fellowship elections my Oxford college caused to be read aloud an Elizabethan statute against bribery,[7] which provided that if any electors contravened the statute their place in the society should be vacant and others elected in their place "as if the said person or persons so offending . . . were naturally dead." This phrase, enunciated with academic relish in the twen-

tieth century, had been borrowed by the sixteenth-century legislator from conveyances creating successive interests in land; and
the clauses in question were intended, without disturbing other
interests, to forfeit the interest of any beneficiary trying to bring
the settlement down.

Roman magistrates similarly sometimes used "as if" clauses in
the formula of direction to a judex, for example telling him to
proceed as if a party had been in possession for the prescription
period. Only one English analogy comes to mind, also coinciden-
tally concerned with prescription. Whereas the Roman device had
been aimed at mischiefs arising because the law of property in
general was falling behind the realities of life, the English mischief
was specific to prescription itself. The acquisition of easements by
long user got into a mess through its notional working. The user
was not seen as creating the easement by its own force: it raised
the presumption that a grant had been made before the time of
legal memory—a date in 1189. That was itself a fiction, and of
course you could not produce evidence that it was not true. But
unreasonable logic allowed you to show that it could not be true
because, for example, the two tenements concerned were in the
same hands until the fourteenth century. The only way then to
give effect to the long user (and avoid the conclusion that a settled state of affairs had throughout been wrongful) was to conjure up a grant made after the disabling situation ended; so judges
encouraged juries to find that there had been a "lost modern
grant," and this was a kind of judicial "as if" legislation. But even
in that seemingly blatant case the inevitable language of "judge-
made" law is misleading: all the judge did was to yield to a "theory" made irresistible by the facts.

A much earlier essentially "as if" fiction will take more explaining. Wrongdoing apart, a claim for a chattel may rest upon
either of two distinct foundations. The claim of bailor against

bailee was at first seen as contractual, arising from the transaction. In the early days of the common law it was not distinguished from the claim of lender against borrower of money; and the borrower of a book, though he came sometimes to be exonerated if he had lost it without any fault in himself,[8] was obviously not exonerated by mere nonpossession any more than was the borrower of money: hence "the bailee's liability." The "proprietary" claim of "owner" against possessor is quite different. The defendant is not liable in this action (though he may have exposed himself to some other action based upon wrongdoing) if he is no longer in possession when the action is brought: the claim of the "owner" as such is always against the person who now has the thing.

By a revealing quirk these distinct claims came to be made under the one writ which came to be known as "detinue."[9] For the bailor this was little more than a change of name from "debt": the bailee was at least prima facie liable, though, unlike the money debtor, he might be allowed to plead loss without any fault. But the owner out of possession seems at first to have had only an imperfectly understood remedy in local courts, and when he needed a writ to bring his claim in a royal court the clerks gave him the same detinue.[10] Nobody at the time would have seen anything odd in this: "Tell the defendant to yield up the thing" was after all exactly what the plaintiff wanted.

The use of the one writ to make the two distinct claims has, however, puzzled historians who assumed that writs were more than just practical orders and somehow represented concepts. A later essay will turn to a more insidious example of this assumption: a writ ordering a feudal lord to "do right" has been taken to be about a kind of ownership known as "the right."[11] But detinue, with its distinct uses, could not be related to any one conceptual basis,[12] and this has some significance outside detinue itself. The assumption that writs reflected legal ideas was related to a more damaging assumption which will feature again in these essays, namely that the "forms of action" of later times were from the beginning the basic entities of the common law.[13] Each kind of claim was seen as having its own appropriate writ, which in turn defined the possible steps in the ensuing lawsuit including the mode of proof; and argument was formal, about fitting this claim into one action rather than another.[14] These were indeed the terms in which lawyers came to think, but they replaced earlier and more rational terms, and the change seems to be associated with the artificialities featured in this essay.

Though initiated by the same writ of detinue, the claims of bailor against bailee and of "owner" against possessor were altogether different, and it followed that the same general issue on the same writ would mean different things depending on the basis relied upon in the plaintiff's statement of claim, his count. The bailor would base his claim on the bailment, and the defendant who waged his law on the general issue just because he no longer had the thing would be perjuring himself. The "owner" out of possession would at first seek to trace the actual steps by which his thing had come to the hands of the defendant, but it became settled that the defendant could not take issue on the detail of those steps but only deny that he was detaining the plaintiff's thing. Attempts to trace the detail were then abandoned: the plaintiff regularly said he had lost the thing and the defendant had found it,[15] and this, at long last, is our fiction.

It served only to specify the nature of the claim, and may have been deliberately chosen for that purpose from its beginning. Instead of seeking to recite the actual facts in one of a range of legally indistinguishable situations, pleaders recited the paradigm case: the finder was the quintessential neutral possessor, neither bailee nor wrongdoer. The fiction (which may sometimes have been true) was no more than a label: in year book language this claim was not "sur bailment" but "sur trover." There was no intention to change the outcome of the particular case, let alone the law generally; and there was no prejudice to the defendant. Provided the action was not by bailor against bailee, any defendant no matter how the thing had come to his possession could properly take the general issue if he no longer had it. But in a later life, to which we shall come, the same fiction was not innocuous for some defendants and indeed played a part in changing the law.[16]

Closer to intentional dishonesty in appearance are fictions affecting jurisdiction. Jurisdiction over an action in what we should call tort at first depended upon the presence or absence of an allegation of breach of the king's peace. It could not come to the king's court without this allegation, and had to come there with it. The allegation also had the effect of excluding the defendant from compurgation and forcing him to jury trial; and, no doubt because compurgation was mistrusted in Westminster (where oath helpers would be strangers rather than neighbors), that exclusion was illogically extended to actions on the case, that is tort actions not making the allegation, when later they became acceptable in the king's courts.[17] In those courts, therefore, all tort actions were tried by jury, a fact central to the development of the common law. The first essay was concerned with the consequent differences between lawsuits in contract and tort in bringing up facts for discussion and so generating rules of substantive law. This essay will later turn to convolutions which resulted in contractual claims being made in tort actions which carried jury trial. But the immediate concern is with the allegation of breach of the king's peace itself. Was it fact, fiction, or just formula?

Whether or not, as has lately been suggested,[18] the wider availability of tort actions in royal courts in the fourteenth century was a conscious governmental response to social difficulties, there is no doubt that at the beginning of that century plaintiffs were alleging breach of the king's peace with no possible basis in the facts. Whether the primary aim was to get royal jurisdiction or to oust the defendant from compurgation (in which case royal jurisdiction was a side effect), this is a fiction by which the plaintiff gains some benefit at the defendant's expense. So why does the defendant not deny it? Effectively he cannot. If he tells the judges it is untrue, they will say the facts are not their business: he should go to the jury with Not Guilty. And if he tells the jury it is untrue, they will not care: they will find for the plaintiff if they think the defendant caused him wrongful harm, without concerning themselves with what they see as a technicality.[19] Developments considered later in this essay will similarly appear to have started in the unpatrolled no-man's-land between the separate concerns of court and jury.

But was even this fiction invented by any plaintiff? In the twelfth and early thirteenth centuries breach of the king's peace was an offense for which the defendant would at least have to buy himself out of prison. A minor fistfight might turn out to be serious if it involved a royal servant or happened on the king's highway. But it might not be clear, for example, where the village green ended and the king's highway began, and in proceedings brought by the victim it was natural that he would first take the benefit of any doubt and then add the allegation anyway if that seemed helpful. The victim of a battery became able to choose between letting his case go to a local court, where it would probably end in compurgation, or getting jury trial in the king's court by adding the magic words. But so far this is all about the same fistfight and the same kind and degree of harm to the victim. It is only when plaintiffs push their luck further that the element of fiction becomes visible.

In 1317 the buyer of a cask of wine got away with assertions that before he could come to collect it the seller had broken into it, drawn off some of the wine and substituted salt water, and all this against the king's peace and with force and arms, to wit with swords and bows and arrows. The defendant just said Not Guilty, and I am sure the jury worried about the wine without giving a thought to the supposed attack in the cellar.[20] But other defendants in similar cases, especially bailees, appealed to the court, not on the factual basis that the allegations were untrue but on the legal basis that they were self-contradictory: one lawfully in possession could not be acting against the king's peace.[21] The first result of that was just to drive such claims underground. One who was actually suing a smith for killing his horse by professional negligence would suppress the relationship. His writ and count were as though against a stranger for killing his horse against the king's peace and once again with the obligatory swords and bows and arrows, and for historians the game may be given away only because defendants are so often called Smith (or Ferrer or Marshal).[22]

At the time, of course, nobody was taken in. So far as the court was concerned the record was straight, and they probably did not even ask what had happened. That was the jury's business. And the jury was still not thinking about the swords and bows and arrows, just about the harm to the plaintiff. And when, by an almost legislative decision of the Chancery, actions for wrongs could go to the king's court without mention of his peace, the relationship could be disclosed and the fiction dropped. The plaintiff would get a writ "on the case" summarizing the actual facts.

But there was no general outbreak of honesty. The honest action against the smith[23] is not accompanied in the king's court by honest actions for battery, omitting mention of the king's peace because the fistfight had not happened on the king's highway or whatever. All that had become unreal. There was no king's peace any more as a distinct entity which could be broken.[24] The victim of the fistfight just chose whether to go for local court and (probably) compurgation or royal court and (certainly) jury trial, and if he made the latter choice he signified it by inserting the appropriate formula. It was no more than a programming code, and nobody now supposed that it had any basis in the facts.

You could give the allegation substantive meaning only by reference to the situations in which you must not use it, for example when the action was avowedly by bailor against bailee. And the ensuing rationalization generated a distinction between trespass and case, and eventually settled on "direct forcible injury" as the essence of trespass and of breach of the king's peace.[25] The end of it was that the whole field of tort got into the king's courts, though artificially divided into the two categories of trespass and case. But in crime there was no relaxation of the original logic. Proceedings for wrongs brought on the king's behalf always had to allege breach of his peace, with the result that theft could be dealt with by the king's courts, but offenses of dishonesty which did not involve a taking were left to wither in local jurisdictions and had later to be recreated in other ways.

So that fiction at least was not an invention made up to produce a desired result. A reality had consequences over jurisdiction and proof. That reality faded away, and its assertion then just programmed the lawsuit to those consequences. Nobody was taken in, and for the most part nobody was harmed. The defendant might have preferred his local court and compurgation, but the only real damage which he could suffer was that breach of the king's peace carried process by way of imprisonment: he could therefore be brought to answer and to pay any damages more quickly. This is a possible explanation of the change whereby the smith, the bailee, and the like could be made to answer in the king's court without the allegation. But if so, it created an inequity in their favor. By that time process by arrest could be had in almost all other personal actions brought in the king's courts, and legislation later extended it to all defendants sued there in tort.[26]

For the purpose of this essay the important result of the fiction and the stretching of its consequences is that all tort actions (except defamation which had to wait until later) could come to the king's court and would there end in jury trial. With contract cases the course of events was entirely different. There was no equivalent of the king's peace, and in principle the king had no interest in such litigation.[27] He created for himself a financial interest in selling writs to plaintiffs, and the eventual result of that was a monetary barrier dividing royal from local jurisdiction in this area.[28] Claims for less than 40 shillings stayed in local courts, for that amount or more went to royal courts. Since that limit was never adjusted for inflation, its mere existence caused a massive shift of jurisdiction to which we shall return.

But, like the king's peace, the limit did provoke evasions. Some plaintiffs rose through the barrier with a trivial tailor-made fiction. One who had sold goods for 32 shillings and wanted royal jurisdiction would have to buy a writ claiming 40 shillings: but if in his statement of claim he recited only the true sale he would lose on the ground that the court had been authorized to hear not a 32-shilling but a 40-shilling claim. If he tried to cure this by asserting untruly that the sale had been for 40 shillings, the defendant could properly wage his law on the general issue. So the plaintiff recited the true 32-shilling sale and threw in a made-up claim for 8 shillings alleged to have been lent, which of course he reckoned to lose.[29] But, unlike alleging breach of the king's peace, this was not a general practice, and even when used it had no consequence beyond the jurisdictional. In particular it brought no advantage to the plaintiff in the matter of proof. Indeed, since compurgation put more pressure on a defendant swearing among his neighbors than in the impersonal Westminster, this would be a motive for breaking downward through the 40-shilling barrier; and in local court records, whether for that reason or just because local litigation was cheaper, one does indeed find claims for a fraction less.[30]

The first of these essays noted that in contract cases in royal courts compurgation remained generally available unless excluded by a document under seal, and our concern then was the effect in preventing the facts from coming out and so slowing the development of contract law. Our present concern is the mechanisms by which change eventually came about. For the well-advised plaintiff who had taken a document under seal there was no need for change, and no change was made. He continued to use the old actions, which he would expect to win. Such hardships as became visible were on the side of the defendant. We saw that a specialty debtor who had paid was still vulnerable to action if he had omitted to retrieve his bond, and that eventually he gained protection in the form of a Chancery injunction obliging the plaintiff to discontinue the action.[31] And it was the same mechanism that protected one who had been induced by fraud to execute a sealed document. These were the principal interventions of equity in the contract field, though it performed one function outside the area of sealed documents, namely in ordering specific performance of certain kinds of agreement after the common law had ceased to do so. But within the common law itself there was no major change, and none of what follows had any application to contracts under seal.

That fact in itself suggests that change was driven largely by the availability of compurgation. By the middle of the seventeenth

century compurgation was out of use, not because means were
found to exclude it from the contract actions but because the contract actions themselves were out of use except when there was a
sealed document. Contractual claims were being made in tort actions which had to go to jury trial even though breach of the
king's peace was not alleged.[32] And all this came to be accompanied by fictions on a larger scale and on their face far more damaging to defendants than that. The defendant in trespass would
not much resent being armed with swords and bows and arrows
which everybody knew were made of paper. But from the seventeenth century to the nineteenth almost every defendant in contract was said to have acted fraudulently. So were lying plaintiffs
persuading juries that their defendants were wicked cheats? Obviously not. But then what were all those allegations there for?

They are evidently a concomitant of the process whereby
plaintiffs, deterred from the old contract actions by their rules
about proof, came to sue in tort instead. And that became possible only when the king's court could hear tort actions without
any allegation about the king's peace. In many cases so coming
in, for example the seller of the wine and the smith,[33] although
the claim is clearly in tort the occasion for the wrong arose out of
an agreement. In the king's court, moreover, what had been a
clear dividing line between the two categories had become
blurred. Tort actions were about past wrongs remediable only by
compensation.[34] But the contract actions, for example the action
of the buyer of services against his defaulting provider, were begun by *praecipe* writs and in principle claimed not compensation
but performance. But the king's courts abandoned attempts to
make the provider of services actually do them (even when he still
could), so that the remedy awarded would be damages as in tort.
And hindsight can see the obliteration of this visible boundary
marker as removing what would have been a major obstacle to

the changes that came about, particularly since juries did not specify the loss which they were compensating and so could award the "wrong" damages—the actual contract damages in what was formally a tort action.

In a famous early case a ferryman undertook to carry the plaintiff's horse across a river but went about it so badly that the horse was drowned. The plaintiff sues in tort and the defendant says it should be (in our terms) contract, for which the contemporary word was *covenant*. He makes that argument because the king's court had adopted a rule requiring plaintiffs suing in covenant to prove the agreement by producing a document under seal, and of course there was none. Covenant just meant agreement, and the writ of that name was limited to claims other than for money or chattels (which would be claimed in debt or detinue and were not conceptualized as arising just from agreement). Covenant was therefore appropriate for agreements to perform services, as on the ferryman's argument in this case, or to convey land. But the ferryman did not have much of an argument: this claim was about killing the horse, not about failing to keep an agreement to get it across the river.[35] And in all similar cases, in which the claim was for damage unrelated to the value of performance, the tort actions were allowed without difficulty and without any thought that the category was being stretched.

Nor was there any difficulty about another kind of tort action arising out of an agreement which could now come to the king's courts. One who bought goods on the basis of a factual assurance by the seller about their quality or the like had his remedy in tort expressly based upon deceit: he had been deceived into paying good money for bad goods. There is evidence that the original remedy in such a case had been rescission;[36] but the king's courts early abandoned specific orders in favor of damages, so this looks like any other tort action. But it had a future which teaches lessons about how law behaves. Because one can be deceived without anybody meaning to deceive him, and because the intention is hard to prove, that action came to depend not upon deceit but upon the assurance having been made formally as a warranty on the sale.[37] The action has in effect moved from tort into contract. There then arose a predictable difficulty: what about the seller who did not warrant but did mean to deceive? Perhaps there should be a separate liability in tort,[38] and in the area of consumer protection the movement to and fro has continued.

The serious difficulty arises if you try to bring an action in tort against one who has simply failed to perform services or convey land as he had agreed. Such attempts are made from the time that tort actions could come in without any talk about the king's peace, and the factual background to most must be sympathetic lawyers trying to help plaintiffs caught out by the royal requirement of a sealed document. You are buying land, a transaction large enough to take you into the king's court (and therefore into the need for a document) for the only time in your life: you have no document and your seller lets you down. Lawyers toyed with various formulations of a complaint sounding in tort; and thoughts of deceit no doubt came naturally to plaintiffs, particularly those who had paid or otherwise done their part in reliance on the promise.

Understanding may be helped by two digressions into modern times. First, the American promissory estoppel comes to the aid of one who has acted to his detriment in reliance on a promise for which he gave no consideration, and the driving sense of injustice arises from his reliance. He does not allege that the other party deceived him, but he feels deceived in the sense of being let down. Second, the modern tort of deceit is limited by the rule that it is about statements rather than promises, and a promise can only constitute an untrue statement if when it was made there was no intention to keep it.[39] But the rule is relatively recent; and its enunciation in the nineteenth century can be seen as following from a process to be mentioned later, namely the reestablishment of a conceptual boundary between tort and contract. Such a boundary had been the basis of clear argument in, for example, the fourteenth-century case of the ferryman.[40] But that clarity was lost, perhaps partly because it could not survive the kind of development we are about to consider; and from the late sixteenth century to the nineteenth argument was about the boundaries not between elementary legal categories but between less rational entities, the various actions.[41]

Now back to the fifteenth century. One disappointed buyer of land made a hard-headed approach, relying upon a very precise idea of deceit.[42] The defendant agreed to sell to the plaintiff and accepted money, but then sold and actually conveyed to a third party. The land was in the suburbs of London, and it is likely that the plaintiff's lawyer practiced in the city courts as well as in Westminster and thought in terms of a sale of city land.[43] In two important respects the city courts had not followed Westminster Hall. They still allowed actions for the enforcement of such agreements without any document under seal,[44] and they still ordered actual performance as the prime remedy. On these facts in the city, therefore, the lack of a sealed document would not have barred the plaintiff from bringing the regular covenant action; but that action would have been pointless since the defendant could not perform. The city, however, had another remedy. It was deceitful of the defendant to accept money and then sell the land to another: and he would be imprisoned until he paid the money back.[45] In the city, therefore, this was visibly a remedy in rescission. The plaintiff's lawyer successfully put the city logic to the royal court; but since that court had limited itself to damages, and did not think in terms of rescission any more than specific performance, the common law was left with an odd-looking result. Without the required document the buyer of land had no remedy in contract, but he could get damages in tort if (but only if) the seller had conveyed to a third party.

For the present purpose it would not be sensible (or easy) to pursue this story further: tort remedies came to be available for mere failure to carry out agreements for services or the sale of land, but at first only if the plaintiff had paid. The case of the land in the suburbs of London is part of that story: and it was brought in to make another point. The talk of deceit in that case was not an invention by the plaintiff's lawyer, not itself a cheat, not the beginning of some conscious fiction.

We now turn to a later chapter in the contract saga, one in which it is tempting, if unrealistic, for the historian to look back from the end of the story to the beginning and imagine a whole profession engaged in just such conscious cheating over half a century and more. By far the commonest contractual claim is the claim for money, the price of the goods or services which were sold. In local courts this was regularly answerable by compurgation, and this was normally open to the defendant in royal courts, though he might choose jury trial. The only way the lender or other prospective plaintiff could exclude compurgation was by taking an acknowledgment of the debt under seal, something that would hardly occur to him unless a large sum was involved. By the end of the sixteenth century the value of money had fallen dramatically, and in particular the value of 40 shillings. The consequence was that debts not large enough for anyone to think of sealing wax were coming in huge numbers to the king's courts in Westminster, and there the defendant could go to compurgation with hired oath helpers and away from the social pressures of his home community.

If hindsight can identify that as the trouble, it can as always see easy solutions. One would have been a statute replacing compurgation with jury trial: but opinion was not all one way, and there was a genuine due-process argument when it was one man's word against another's. Another would have been a statute returning small cases to local courts by indexing the 40-shilling limit, but of course nobody was thinking in those terms: what people saw was prices now rising, not the value of money regularly falling. Another would have been to require law waged in Westminster to be actually made in the local community, so that the oath helpers, like a *nisi prius* jury, would be neighbors. Yet another would have been to make compurgation in Westminster more effective, and it may be no coincidence that a procedure about which little is known makes fitful appearances about this time. Nothing was done about the oath helpers, but the defendant about to make his law was himself examined and admonished before he swore his oath.[46] In the preceding essay we saw this precipitating the enunciation of a substantive rule, namely that the balance of a debt could not be forgiven on the acceptance of a lesser sum.[47] But only the scrupulous defendant doubtful about his liability in law would disclose such facts, and the pervasive difficulty arose from the unscrupulous anxious to evade liability however clear in law.

These easy solutions of hindsight are unreal because they postulate a single mind addressing an identified problem, and we totally misunderstand legal history whenever we think in such terms. Compurgation ceased to be available because plaintiffs were advised to bring actions in which it was not permitted. In time this came to be done on purpose, but the early steps which made it possible were not taken with that end in mind. They were genuine complaints of damage resulting from reliance on a promise of payment, which was quite distinct from a claim for the payment itself. A brewer's business was damaged when a quantity of malt was not delivered as promised, and his action for that damage was obviously distinct from the action he might have brought to claim the malt—which would have been the same action as that for a money debt.[48]

When money debts were indeed involved such claims were less obviously distinct and, for the future, much more important. We will follow only one of the merging streams in this development. Our plaintiff is a merchant who lives by his credit, and who presses his defendant for the £5 he is owed. The defendant is in a temporary difficulty but faithfully promises to pay the £5 at a stated future date. Relying on that promise—and in a mercantile community one does rely on such promises—the plaintiff makes other bargains with third parties which he intends to meet from the promised £5. When the defendant lets the plaintiff down, the plaintiff lets the third parties down; and this causes him loss of credit to the actual value of £500, which his claim inflates to £1000. He sues, not for the relatively trivial debt but for the ruinous reliance damage, and he uses the language of deceit. In the years around the middle of the sixteenth century, such claims seem to be genuine.[49] Near the end of the century, it is clear that the tort action is being used to recover the debt, and that the loss of mercantile credit arising from transactions with third parties is fictitious. The third parties now have names of the order of Doe and Roe, and the choice of names for them can sometimes be correlated with the attorneys acting for plaintiffs.[50]

So, as with the king's peace, the fiction was not invented. It is the residue of a reality, and the question for us is how the reality disappeared. Once again the answer can only lie in the dark of the jury room. Our example supposed a debt of £5 and actual damage to credit of £500, though a higher figure would be claimed. In their private discussions the jury find that the plaintiff was so damaged to the extent of £500; but then, with no lawyers present to get in the way of their own common sense, they throw in the amount of the debt and award damages of £505. There is, however, no itemization: outside the jury room there is nothing to show how this blank total was reached. When lawyers realize what is happening, it becomes possible to use the tort action to recover the debt and so oust the defendant from compurgation. And the jury will award whatever they think is actually due, without worrying about the alleged damage to credit unless it was real, and perhaps without worrying about the reality of the promise to pay as something separate from the transaction raising the debt.

But the final result is as untidy as the reasoning. Formally the debt had not been in issue and had not been paid within the damages; so the plaintiff can sue again in the regular debt action, and strictly the defendant will be perjuring himself if even then he goes to compurgation on the unspoken basis that he has now paid. A great dispute and a considerable scandal developed, largely because the facts were lost in a general issue on which the judges of the two principal courts gave opposite directions:[51] did the jury have to find that there had been a real promise to pay separate from the transaction raising the debt? The dispute came to a head in a case in which a special verdict was taken: the defendant owed but had given no separate undertaking to pay. The end, still grudging and untidy, was an acknowledgment that the plaintiff in the tort action might recover not only his damages, if any, but also the debt;[52] and the one action was to bar the other. Even this still left another difficulty to be settled. The logic of the tort action was that the plaintiff had relied upon the defendant's promise to pay some preexisting debt, and it made no difference how that debt had arisen, whether out of a loan, a sale of goods, or anything else. But it obviously mattered to the defendant when the promise was a fiction and the action was really for the debt it-self. So the courts came to disallow such claims unless minimum particulars were given. The tort action was now being conscious-ly manipulated to do the contract job.[53]

"A sensible, practical view it may be; but legal principle avenges itself." This was the comment of the greatest of legal his-torians on the solution to a very different problem,[54] but it could be written on almost every page of any history of the common law. Even on the practical level getting rid of compurgation was not all to the good. The oaths of unscrupulous defendants gave way to the manipulation of juries by unscrupulous plaintiffs, for which the Statute of Frauds[55] prescribed a dismal remedy. And if the rules of proof governing early contract actions did not always work well, they were clearer in purpose and effect than the main product of these twists, namely the "doctrine" of consideration. On the conceptual level, although lawyers were not now thinking in those terms, the boundary between contract and tort was per-manently displaced. The original idea of covenant (as we have seen, the medieval equivalent of our contract) was distinct, about performance or the value of performance. Harm arising from bad performance or deceit or the like was quite different, to be com-pensated in actions based upon wrongdoing. These all ended up in a woollier idea of contract as being about compensation for al-most all kinds of harm arising in the vicinity of an agreement.

In the development of crime and tort, the first of these essays conjured up a dialogue between judges and jurors. Ideas of right and wrong originated from the jurors and were formulated by judges into substantive rules of law. The rules were, so to speak, not so much made by judges as drafted by them; and the result had always to be acceptable to jurors, which is another way of saying that the law had to be acceptable to its lay subjects. In that process the only fiction involved on any scale was that of the

king's peace, and it hardly obstructed the dialogue: one early con-
scientious jury did try to say the defendant had done the deed but
not with force and arms and was ignored.[56] Thereafter the king's
peace was just accepted as a lawyers' formula, and the dialogue
generated a coherent if untidy law of wrongs.

Getting remedies in contract out of actions for wrongs was a
less tidy matter. In the case of money debts we followed one line
of development which started with a genuine claim for a wrong,
the damage flowing from reliance on the promise to pay; and it
was commonsense woolly minded jurors who unwittingly took
the important first step in the use of that claim to recover money
debts. Probably nobody expected them to include the amount of
the debt in the damages. More important, there was nothing to
show that was what they had done. Judges could hardly have objected even if they had wanted to, and in the end of course they
did not want to. More or less willingly they accepted a fudge
which was not of their own making.[57]

But what would the jurors' common sense have made of all
that followed? First, on the general issue, opposing judges were
giving them opposite directions about the need for a promise separate from the transaction raising the debt. Then one jury in the
climactic case was allowed (or persuaded) to return a special verdict: indebted but no separate promise, and that was taken to be
sufficient for the plaintiff. Thereafter lawsuits resumed their normal pattern, going to the general issue of *Non assumpsit*—he did
not promise. Of course the defendant did not promise, but the
jury would have to find that he did if the plaintiff was to recover
his debt. It is an awkwardness to which we shall return.[58].

The story of the devious recovery of money debts has a twin
in a devious action which, similarly to preclude wager of law, replaced the old action claiming specific chattels. We saw earlier
that the one writ of detinue enforced two totally distinct liabili-

ties, so that the same general issue would mean different things depending on the basis relied on in the plaintiff's count.[59] For the finder or other neutral possessor, whose liability to the "owner" stemmed solely from his possession, the general issue meant that he was not now detaining the plaintiff's property; and if he had been in possession but was so no longer, he could honestly wage his law. The bailee, whose liability stemmed from the transaction, could not. Unlike the money debtor, he might possibly have an affirmative special plea of loss without fault; but the general issue should mean the equivalent for him as for the money debtor: either that there had been no bailment or that the thing had been returned.

Now suppose either knowingly sold the goods and pocketed the proceeds. The "finder" will not be liable in detinue because, albeit wrongfully, he is no longer in possession. So he must be reached in an action based on the wrong; and in that tort action the plaintiff comes to borrow from detinue the old allegation of loss and finding precisely to show that detinue would be no remedy for him.[60] It is still just a conventional label covering a range of legally indistinguishable situations, and the "fiction" is no more harmful to the defendant than the truth would be.

But suppose it is bailee who wrongfully sells the goods. He cannot honestly take the general issue in detinue which is therefore bailor's proper remedy; but, like the simple contract debtor, bailee can risk his soul and win the action by waging his law on the general issue. If bailor seeks to avert wager by bringing the tort action, and truthfully recites the bailment, he will be told that he should be bringing detinue. So he suppresses the bailment and makes the standard assertion of loss and finding. This had generally been untrue for more than a century, but just as a known label denoting possession otherwise than as bailee. To paste that label over what really was a bailment was indeed a fiction that mattered: it deprived the defendant of his right to answer by wager. So could the defendant in this one situation deny what in all other situations everybody knew to be a fiction? Hindight can see that detinue, like debt on a simple contract, had to go. The detailed story of its replacement is too convoluted for this essay, but it provides two texts for a relevant sermon. A fiction that has become uncomfortably blatant may be rationalized into a constructive truth. When bailee wrongfully disposed of the goods and bailor (in order to bring the tort action) charged him not as bailee but as finder, this was legitimated by incantation: bailee's wrongful action was said to have "determined the bailment." Worse was to follow. If detinue with its wager of law was to be entirely replaced, the tort action had to be made available even against a defendant (whether bailee or "finder") who still had the object. Hitherto the wrong, the "conversion,"[61] had involved a real event such as a sale. Now a slogan turned it into a metaphysical event: although mere failure to return the object could only be a detinue, juries were directed that an unequivocal refusal without specific reason could be a sufficient "denial of the plaintiff's title" to amount to a conversion.[62]

There is a third and more famous text for the same sermon. The theoretical basis of the tort action replacing debt was reliance on a promise to pay. That promise came invariably to be fictitious, but in terms it was what was denied by the general issue, and if the plaintiff was to recover his debt the jury would have to find that the defendant had promised. This conjured up the best-known of these whitewashing slogans: "Every contract executory imports in itself an assumpsit"[63] means simply that any debtor is presumed to promise to pay.[64] In all these cases the resort to whitewash suggests that lawyers were having qualms about the integrity of their results. In the last case in particular it may also have been that jurors needed to be persuaded (or at any rate comforted) about the veracity of their sworn verdicts: if they found the defendant owed the money they were told to find that he had promised to pay even though they had also been told it did not matter if he had not in fact promised.

But for lawyers it was not the fictions as such that needed legitimation so much as the use of one action where another was proper, the replacement of debt and detinue by actions on the case. Until recently the "forms of action" were seen as the original entities of the common law, and development from the beginning was perceived as a series of struggles to bring factual situations within the scope of one action rather than another. When lawyers were indeed thinking in those terms, argument was about largely irrational boundaries and integrity was more a formal than an intellectual matter.

But this mechanical vision of legal argument was not aboriginal. "Trespass" and "covenant" began not as the names of actions but as elementary categories of the nature of "tort" and "contract." For a time those categories simply disappeared, so that *covenant* for example became the name of an action and associated with documents under seal, and the word most nearly representing our "contract" was *assumpsit*. The shift in legal thinking has not been traced in detail, and the detail may not be easy to recover. The main cause (perhaps the sole cause) must have been the loss by *trespass* of its original wide sense of wrong,[65] but it may well be that a contributory part was played by the developments we have been considering. To replace debt and wager with *indebitatus assumpsit* and jury trial was questionable enough to call for whitewash. But it was less unacceptable than the same result flying its true colors: a contractual complaint being remedied by giving the "wrong" damages in a tort action.

So these "substantive" fictions grew as part of the process whereby new results came to be reached not by changing the old answers but by asking new questions, setting up the disputes in different terms within different legal categories or different "forms of action." As between tort and contract, while the result has been a curiously amorphous law of contract, perhaps no great harm has been done. As between tort and property the main casualty may indeed be the "action of trover" for the "tort of conversion." The tort action could do the proprietary job only by expelling any element of wrongdoing; and since any "denial of title" could amount to a conversion odd results followed. In an extreme case the owner could recover the full value of his chattel from an innocent auctioneer whose "denial of title" consisted only in arranging the sale and who gained nothing but his commission.[66]

The legal historian necessarily looks at developments over long periods, and one of the mistakes he can easily make is to endow the lawyers who took part with his own vision, able from the beginning to see the end, perhaps even to aim at it. Nobody ever invented a fiction as a dodge to get a tort remedy in a contract situation. Until each development was well advanced, indeed, probably nobody saw that that was happening. The creditor who contracted other obligations in reliance on his debtor's promise to pay was not after the debt: he really was suing for the loss of the mercantile reputation on which his livelihood depended. The true innovators here were first the jurors who innocently included the amount of the debt in an unexplained award of damages and then the lawyers who took increasingly blatant advantage on behalf of later creditors. Last came the judges who, some gladly and some not, accepted a major change in "the law" they could never have brought about for themselves. And even then the intellectual nature of the change had to be blurred: it was not a boundary between contract and tort that had been surmounted but just a boundary between "forms of action."

III
MANAGEMENT, CUSTOM, AND LAW

BECAUSE ENGLISH RECORDS REACH BACK TO a true starting point, the first of these essays was able to describe the mechanisms by which the common law of crime and tort, and up to a point contract, came to be stated in substantive terms. Procedural developments compelled the consideration of facts, and the first of these was the substitution of human decision for supernatural tests of oaths denying liability generally. And it seems more likely than not that the Roman law also began with the replacement of supernatural tests by human decision, though at a time before the earliest evidence. In both systems the process generating most substantive legal statement was that of direction or advice given to laymen by magistrates or judges. But it was slow.

This essay is concerned with the very different process by which the common law of property in land came into being, and though nothing suggests universality, it may not be unique. Its essence, the development of abstract rights from customary claims against some controlling authority, seems a priori likely. The Roman law of property is entirely coherent, but it is based on an idea of ownership which appears to be mystical in itself and the formalities of the action claiming ownership in the important kinds of property express no rational basis for the claim, unless it is significant that the claim is to be owner "according to the law of the knights."[1] But you can live with mysticism if you have rules, as did the developed Roman law, which made you owner if you had been in possession (of course subject to predictable conditions) for a relatively short period of time.

Even analytical jurisprudence, in the days when there was such a discipline, never got far with ownership, and linguistic usage is no help. Possessive adjectives may have no legal content at all, as in "I missed my train." And in "I was cheated out of my inheritance" it is important to remember that the inheritance may never have belonged to the speaker any more than the train did: a hope or expectation had just been disappointed. If his complaint had any basis, he may have supposed that somebody had been under some obligation to give him the inheritance. And even when the possessive does have legal content, what is "mine" is often not property but the benefit of an obligation as in "my job," "my money in the bank," "my hotel room."

The first of these essays began from the ambivalence of a bailment between obligation and property.[2] For the writer of *Bracton* the difference between lending money and lending a specific object was obvious, but only because he had read of it in Roman books. In the English courts of his day it was still hidden within the supernatural test of a blank denial of liability when lender sued borrower, and it began to emerge only at the end of the thirteenth century when facts began to emerge in lawsuits and human deciders had to wrestle with such matters as the bailee having without fault lost the thing.[3] That is an early chapter in the emergence of the common law of property in chattels (such as it is), essentially questions of right and wrong between equals, and the mechanisms were those described in the first of these essays. That clear answers were slow to emerge did not greatly matter because chattels were only a matter of money, and generally not very much money. Nobody's way of life or livelihood was at stake.

Land was livelihood—until relatively modern times almost everyone's livelihood—and the law relating to it started as the detailed arrangements of most of daily life, doing in particular the work that we associate with labor law and contracts of employment on the one hand and with family provision on the other. Rules were not teased out in luxurious centuries of litigation: order was essential from the beginning, and started not as a matter of what we would call rules of law but as the criteria of a management in control.

Those criteria were the customs which the management had found it expedient or felt obliged to follow. The part played by custom in legal development used to be much discussed, often on the unrealistic basis that what ordinary people ordinarily do somehow congeals into law. A great Columbia legal historian wrote a sentence worth quoting even out of context: "Such a 'custom' may have been a folkway but it was the way of the folk in power."[4] The customs from which the common law developed were not the habits of ordinary people but the norms followed by governing bodies with power of decision. It follows from what was said in the preceding essays that in most legal areas the customs of customary courts were not substantive but procedural, about the ex post facto settlement of disputes. But ex post facto is too late for the arrangements of life. On the death of a landholder, for example, there had to be known criteria for deciding who was to succeed him in the land and, at first more important, in the duties that went with the land.

Some homely modern analogies may help understanding of what follows. Perhaps the most tenacious of managerial criteria is that of Buggins's Turn. Inns of Court have long elected a new head every year, and the almost invariable custom was that the senior man who had not yet served would be elected. Most Oxford and Cambridge colleges have real elections for a Master or Warden who will be there many years: but my old Oxford college changed its subwarden every year, and similarly always elected the senior man who had not yet done it. You could see disaster coming, and it came: but it was not much of a disaster, usually limited to embarrassing speeches on formal occasions. The custom would not arise for an office carrying power to do real damage, and it preserves comity within an institution which has become externally secure. But if there arise new dangers with which the officer will have to cope, you may have to hurt Buggins and face internal discord by electing the most suitable and not the most senior man. Buggins's Turn was never a rule which directly gave Buggins the position. It was just a custom influencing the electors: and the election itself made the officer.

A schoolboy recollection comes to mind. It was a large boarding school in which each boy was assigned to one of a number of houses. Each house had, say, ten studies, allocated at the absolute discretion of the housemaster; but, again for reasons of comity, he regularly went by seniority. At the beginning of his last year the tenth boy confidently expects to have a study: but on the housemaster's list he has been passed over in favor of the eleventh. Whatever the reason—better conduct, greater need, favoritism, or simple mistake—the tenth obviously has no direct claim against the eleventh boy. Equally obviously the eleventh boy, however uncomfortable his position, has no property right that he can yield up to the tenth. All either can do is ask the housemaster to reallocate the study. Possessive adjectives may be bandied about: but there are no rights at all, only the allocations of the housemaster's list.

Autobiography continues. From that school the writer went to Cambridge where one of his professors was well into his eighties, having taken office before a retiring age was imposed. And another analogy will fit more closely if set in those days. The professor of astrobiology dies. For each of their established chairs Oxford and Cambridge maintain a standing board of electors so that when a vacancy occurs no argument arises over who is to make the choice. The astrobiology board is convened and elects Dick, and the usual outcry ensues. All but the electors agree that Dick is no good. Less usually (but it helps the argument) they agree also that the one obvious man for the job was Harry. But there is nothing Harry or his supporters can do except grumble. Suppose they grumble so loudly that the university authorities (unthinkably) agree that the electors got it wrong: what can the university then do for Harry? What it cannot do is get rid of Dick. He has been duly elected and has tenure, and he can be dismissed only by due process for some wrongdoing on his part. The only possible thing they could do would be to create a second chair of astrobiology personal to Harry, also of course for life.

Instead of grumbling, could one imagine Harry going to court? Obviously he could not claim the chair from Dick, as though it were somehow "his." However clearly the customary criteria had pointed to Harry, Dick had been elected. Any claim would have to be against the university. Even today one can hardly imagine an English tribunal intervening for Harry. But it is not unthinkable that they might do so for Harriet. And conceivably cases based on discrimination might turn the customary criteria into rules so clear that Harry himself would in the end have a remedy. What remedy? Even if the tribunal goes so far as to say that the university must do now what it should have done in the first place and give the established chair to Harry, Dick still has tenure, is still entitled to be professor for life; and perhaps the university must again create a new personal chair, this time for Dick.

Can one really imagine a management controlling land so absolutely that rights in it were as dependent as those of the schoolboys in their studies? Well yes. Some Japanese magnates were certainly in that position. And those school studies are like the examination problem the law teacher struggles to make up, knowing that real life may raise his point far more neatly. Down to 1925 much English land was still classed as "copyhold," so named because the only document of title you could have was a copy of the appropriate entry in (as it were) the housemaster's list. This list was the record of the manor court. Copyholders derived from unfree tenants of manors whose personal unfreedom was nothing like slavery, but whose tenements had been held in return for such agricultural labor as the lord required and who held in some sense at his will. Most lords exercised their will rigidly according to the customs of the manor. The tenant was secure so long as he did what was required, and could be confident that when he died his son would succeed him. But it was not the custom that would directly give his son the tenement: it was a decision of the lord's court duly noted in its record. Similarly the tenant might in fact be able to alienate to a person of his own choosing; but that would take the form of his surrendering his tenement to the lord who would admit the new man instead. And this surrender and admittance would equally be noted on the court's record, which served as a definitive register of title long after it represented any real exercise of the lord's will or any actual decision by a manorial court.

What we are describing is an authority sovereign within its own sphere but holding to its own customs. The custom points to the decision, but what has legal effect is the decision actually made. If the authority has departed from its own custom, for example by not admitting the son when the tenant dies, there is nothing the son can do about it. The only factor which can change that is the existence of a superior jurisdiction willing to interfere at his instance, and we shall see that the key change in the development of the common law of property in land was precisely the willingness of royal jurisdiction to override the decisions of lesser feudal courts. For freehold land this change largely followed from the regular provision of new royal remedies in the twelfth century: but those remedies were not made available to tenants at the level of unfree tenure. The obligations of such a tenant were still too much a matter of discretion to be set out as fixed conditions of his tenure, which itself therefore had to remain discretionary, a matter of managerial control. Not until much later did tenants at that level gain their own roundabout means of protection in royal courts. Until then they remained a working model of a system of customary allocation.

To the extent that the common law developed an idea of ownership of land, the key element was inheritance. If when you die there are rules designating someone as your heir and passing title to him by their own force, it is natural to see an ownership passing automatically from one generation to the next. And the automatic nature of the transmission astonishingly persisted in England until 1897,[5] by which time of course inheritance had long been seen as just a form of intestate succession. In that year statute required freehold land to reach the heir through the personal representatives, but formerly title had passed directly to the heir without even official authentication. He just assumed control, and there would be no authoritative pronouncement unless a rival claim was pursued to judgment—and even then the judgment would not identify an "owner," only declare which of these two parties had the greater right. And since the rules designating who was heir had to deal with all possible combinations of relationship and survival, they were complicated. They could not possibly have been formed in a sky as abstract as that in which they seemed to operate, directly passing title from the dead to the living and subject only to the possibility of litigation ex post facto. They were not formed in that way of course. They started as the customary criteria applied in the court of a feudal lord when "appointing" one to succeed his dead tenant. More specifically the common law rules started as the criteria for the choice of successor on the death of a tenant by knight service. After the Conquest great men came to hold great lands in return for providing a quota of fighting men for the king, and they came to satisfy this obligation by making downward grants of some of their lands to lesser men who would provide part of the quota or to individuals who would themselves serve. It turned out that this was not a reliable way for the king to raise an army, and actual military service faded first into money payments and then into oblivion. But the structure and its associated customs persisted. They had mostly come to England with the Conqueror, having first taken shape on an unstable continent in the context of weaker men bringing themselves and their lands under the protection of a stronger man to form a secure unit for which they must all be ready to fight. On the death of a tenant in such a context the choice of successor would obviously be influenced by his fitness for the fighting job.

Let us go back to institutions electing their officers on the basis of Buggins's Turn. You would not have developed the custom if the office was such that an incompetent holder might bring harm to the institution, and if new dangers arise you may pass Buggins over. For the purpose of inheritance in twelfth-century England and thereafter, the part of Buggins was played by the dead man's eldest son. He was the obvious candidate: but the early evidence suggests that he was not always chosen. On the death of one of his barons, King Henry I is said to have passed over the elder son in favor of the son of a later marriage because he was the better knight.[6] The particular story may or may not be true, but it would not have been told unless such a happening was thinkable. Perhaps in the same reign an elder son was certainly passed over because he was somehow incapable; and at the time I am sure the younger was accepted by all as having the only title there was, and on his death the land would pass to his heir. Later there was a sequel to which we shall come.[7]

Nor is it merely that you may depart from your custom when the individual it designates seems unsuitable. Your custom will itself reflect likely suitability. Take a doubt which seems to have reflected divergent practice in different European lordships. When the tenant dies he leaves a living younger son and a grandson by a dead elder son. Some favored the latter as representing our Buggins. But he is more likely than his uncle to be an infant not yet capable of doing the service, and if service is what you need you may regularly choose the uncle. In England the king's courts seem always to have favored the grandson. But for a long time they had to fudge their answer because the royal title itself was affected. King John had been the younger brother of Richard I, who left no legitimate issue; and an intervening brother now dead had left a boy and a girl. John, in the words of a modern biographer, "saw to" the boy; but the girl lived on, an honored but unmarried prisoner and an embarrassment.[8]

It follows that the less the duties matter the more likely it is that the custom will become inflexible, and will itself provide solutions for common difficulties like infancy. What were you to do if your tenant died leaving a very young son? There was a time at which it was at least thinkable to pass the boy over. Within thirty years of the Conquest a military tenant so died, and his brother argued that the lord should now grant the land to him. The lord felt himself committed to the boy, even though he could not yet do the service due, and the brother was refused. But it was a possible thing for him to ask, and since somebody had to do the service the land was granted to the brother to hold in his nephew's name for the duration of the infancy.[9] Some such arrangement may for a time have been the norm, and for lesser nonmilitary tenures the dues and services of an infant tenant continued to be done by fiduciary guardians on the infant's behalf.

But for military tenures, as the service became a less important consideration, a different custom grew up. The lord would retain the land in his own hand and himself take its revenues (subject to provision for the infant), and only when the heir came of age would the lord take his homage and deliver seisin of "his" inheritance. As between the king and his tenants-in-chief this remained the regular course.[10] But for lesser lords of military tenures there was a further change: the king required them to acknowledge the infant as tenant by taking his homage and delivering seisin before assuming real control of the land.[11] And that control, beneficial possession of land of which the infant was already seised, was the classical "wardship" of the common law, becoming more valuable than the increasingly unwanted service and a main economic component of lordship.

A boy will grow up, but if the tenant leaves only a daughter she will never be able to fight, and it seems clear that there was a time at which she could transmit a claim to her issue but was not herself seen as capable of inheriting. What came to happen was that the lord would find her a husband who would serve for life as his substitute man, as it were a surrogate heir to bridge the tenurial gap.[12] It was a way of giving a chance to her issue while providing immediately for the service. And when later their tenurial bearings are forgotten and these things come to be perceived in terms of pure property, the widower's "curtesy," his continuing tenure for life of all his dead wife's lands, will be contrasted with the widow's right to dower of a third of her dead husband's as though the two arrangements were comparable—just the unequal "marital estates" of surviving spouses.

So far then we are looking at customs which are seen as concerned as much with the filling of a vacant post as with the devolution of property. What has custom to say about the position of the appointee? First, he is in principle appointed for life. The word "homage" reminds us that the lord was not originally granting property but buying a man and allocating the tenement by way of payment so long as the man lived. There were no social security or pension schemes, and few men lived into the incapacities of old age. But the early evidence does show some resigning, typically asking the lord to accept the heir apparent now so that in effect the inheritance happens in the tenant's lifetime.[13] At the upper levels of society the retired tenant might buy his way into a monastery to arrange for his hereafter; and at the peasant level, where the services more often continued to matter so that retirement was common, village houses might have what we would call a granny-flat.[14] Tenants as well as lords perceived the arrangement as a position carrying duties as well as rights, not as simple property.

If the tenant is in for life, can he be dismissed? He can of course: in its own sphere this governing body is sovereign. But the custom is that he has tenure like the professor, and may be deprived only for some wrong on his part such as a failure of service. That should be done not at the lord's will but by judgment of his court. The court would consist of fellow tenants, the defaulter's peers.[15] Its due process started with a series of summonses; then chattels would be taken by way of security; and if the defaulter still did not come the land would be taken, at first again by way of security to make him come and answer; and finally he might be deprived, disseised. But the implications of this will be postponed to the following essay, where the changing connotations of *seisin* and *disseisin* will be explored.

So the lord gave seisin to the tenant who then had tenure. Subject to the possibilities of the tenant resigning or being deprived by due process for some wrong, he would remain in seisin until he died. But that was the end of it. This was a realistic world in which you could not take the land with you and there was no abstract entity which could pass from one generation to the next. When this man dies, nobody else will be seised until the lord seises him. The lord must make a like arrangement with a new man, who in turn will hold the tenement for life. The customs of inheritance indicate to the lord and his court who the new man should be, and the one so designated may think that he has a right to the tenement, may even speak of "my" inheritance. But in the lord's court nothing is his until he is actually given it. His "right" is no more than an expectation which in that sovereign body may be disappointed, just as the obvious candidate for the professorship may be passed over by the electors.

But if the body ceases to be sovereign the particular situation of the expectant heir and the general perception of inheritance are transformed. Suppose that the lord and his court for whatever reason put in the wrong man who does homage to the lord. Like the duly elected professor, that wrong man has tenure; and if the king's court later makes the lord accept the man he should have chosen, it will also make him compensate the man he did in fact choose, giving him land of equal value. The procedure for securing this right to compensation, known as "voucher to warranty" remains common in the thirteenth century: what the loser had was very obviously just the benefit of an obligation.

But what the winner has looks increasingly like property. We go back to a case mentioned earlier.[16] At a time when the customs of inheritance were still just criteria for lords' courts, one

Bernard died leaving an elder son who was somehow incapable, and the land was granted to the younger. At the time I am sure this was seen as a proper exercise of discretion within the custom, not a defiance of it. Anyway the decision was final, and was not seen as about anything like ownership: the question was just whom to put in now. Similarly when the younger son died, his son was put in by the lord in normal accordance with the custom. But then, half a century and more later, the grandson of that elder son who had been passed over makes a claim in the king's court. He says, truly, that he is now Bernard's heir: a kind of ownership is being asserted.

The important changes flow from the change of jurisdiction. The lord's court had customs indicating the proper exercise of its discretion. But the king's court could not think in terms of discretion: there could only be fixed rules. Fit or not, it had to be the eldest son, and even the exception may be significant. A leper kept land he held at the onset of his affliction but (according to *Bracton*)[17] could not later succeed as heir: inheritance was not the passive and private accrual of an abstract title but a transaction normally before witnesses and involving the parties in the physical act of homage. More important, in the lord's court the customs were about a present choice which when made was final. The king's court is undoing a choice which has been made, and, in such a case as that of the descendants of Bernard, made long ago. Suddenly we have all the phenomena of property, including the inherent mischief that lawyers have ever since had to wrestle with in many different contexts. A legal title can exist in the sky unaffected by events on the ground, and may later be brought down to defeat expectations legitimately flowing from what has since actually happened.

But the change of tense was not obvious at the time and has been missed by historians. Even the canons of inheritance themselves could have been written out after the change in the same words as before it. It is just that what started as customary criteria for a present choice have become rules of law which can be brought to bear on choices made in the past. More follows. If those now holding under the past choice can be defeated, then the choice was without effect. There is now only that title existing in the king's court. Lords long continue to take what one may call a consequential homage, but this cannot add much to the title of the rightful heir, only attract a liability on the lord to warrant if he has accepted the wrong man. The lord is gradually extruded from the idea of inheritance, leaving that gap which would not be even partially filled until 1897 when his long-forgotten part was in some sense taken by the personal representatives. During the intervening centuries nobody gave anything to the new tenant or did anything to certify his entitlement: there was that title in the sky descending indefinitely by its own autonomous magic. The lord had been made redundant and his part in the routine of inheritance automated.

The basic ideas of the developed land law can best be understood as the residue left when the controlling lord disappeared from a system of ideas to which he had been central. Suppose that a lord, still very much in control, granted land to a bastard (whose important characteristic in the present context is that he could have no heirs except his own legitimate issue). The bastard went to the Holy Land and is known to have died there. What is not known is that on the way he married and begot a son. The lord assumes that the tenement is not only vacant but at his free disposal, and he makes a fresh grant to a new tenant and later to that new tenant's heir. Then the legitimate heir of the bastard turns up. His claim to the land is essentially against the lord: "You seised my father and took his homage and so bound yourself to renew the arrangement with his heir, and I am his heir."

But the present tenant has an identical claim. Both have obligations enforceable against the lord, but both obligations concern the one tenement to which, on these facts, the bastard's heir will be said to have the "greater right." The comparative adjective is needed because the loser has a right too, but has to be content with land of equal value. Only when there is no controlling authority, when the lord has been dissolved out from the terms of thought, will the right be seen as a sort of abstract ownership, and the greater right that which is derived from the earlier seisin, itself seen as a kind of abstract possession.

But just as nobody ever noticed the changed operation of the canons of inheritance, so did nobody ever notice the concomitant change in the sense of "the right": a claim to be chosen to fill a present vacancy has become a kind of ownership which can override a choice made in the past. And there was of course an associated change in the sense of "seisin." Consideration of that, however, will be postponed to the following essay as a more fundamental illustration of the way in which the law can hide great changes behind unchanging words.

Nor were "the right" and "seisin" the only mystical residues left when a superior jurisdiction first controlled and then dissolved out the original management. Concepts may be confusing but are not in themselves harmful. The same cannot be said of the labyrinthine complexities of future interests. A vestige of realism remains of course: you still cannot take it with you. But now you can control what you must leave behind. The old management has been automated, and today's owner can program his property so that it will pass automatically to successive beneficiaries, and it may be far in the future before anyone is again owner as fully as he is. There is something perverse in a system which permits such settlements and then has to develop a separate "rule against perpetuities" to prevent their reaching too far into the future. In the words of the man chiefly responsible for that rule, such arrangements "fight against God."[18]

But they grew from things that a management in control might sensibly do. Let us go back yet again to that twelfth-century Bernard who left a somehow incapable elder son.[19] The lord just passed the elder over and gave the land to the younger, and thereafter he followed the usual custom and gave it to the younger son's heir. But instead he might on Bernard's death have given it to the younger with the expressed intention that when the younger died he as lord would then give it not to the heir of the younger but to the heir of the elder. There is nothing out of the way about a management in control saying what it would do in the future, and doing it when the time came. But the same factual result has a magical look when there is no management, when its function has been automated so that a grant is programmed from the beginning to one person for life with remainder to another.

But even if there is a disturbing touch of magic, the remainder after a life estate is not unreasonable. It was from arrangements within the family that the legal monsters grew. We saw that the customs governing the choice of heir were largely directed to getting somebody fit to do the lord's service, and we did not even mention the most obtrusive result, namely that the entire holding must go to a single heir. The eldest son would take all to the exclusion of younger sons and daughters. And, as service diminishes in importance and land is increasingly seen as just property, tension grows between this result and the wish to provide for other family members.

Suppose that a man having military tenants holding of him is also a father with three sons and a daughter. When he dies, his superior lord will grant all his land to the eldest son. This will include the land held by the military tenants, but the son will be bound by the homage they had done to honor their position: they will become his tenants as they had been his father's. And since the service they owe him goes toward the service he owes the superior lord, they are a self-balancing item in his accounts. But so long as service matters, any free allocation the father makes to his daughter or younger sons will diminish his ability to do the remainder of the service he owes to the superior lord. So long as he lives that is his business: he is making not an out-and-out gift but what a later age would call an allowance, and he has the managerial ability to adjust it as his accounts require. And if he leaves things like that until he dies, the eldest son may in what will then be his managerial discretion continue the arrangement. Or he may not—and commonly did not. So the father's real problem is precisely in making the arrangement proof against his heir.

In the case of the daughter custom, with independent backing from the Church, obliged the eldest son and his heirs after him (that is the holders for the time being of the father's inheritance) to honor an allowance made to the daughter and her husband on marriage, provided that it was of only an appropriate share of the inheritance, and provided that after two or three generations the arrangement would lose its character as an allowance. The then heir of the daughter would do homage to the then heir of the eldest son, and the land would be held for full service in the same way as that held by the other military tenants. It would cease to be a drain and become another self-balancing item in the family inheritance.

For the present purpose, however, it was a younger son who did the damage. Any allocation to him would be effective in the father's lifetime: but custom imposed no obligation on the heir to maintain it. The reason given by our main source is that fathers were too fond of their younger sons and would leave too little for heirs.[20] The background is no doubt that of the biblical Benjamin: the gift to the younger son is procured by his mother, the present wife; and the heir had been born of an earlier marriage. The only thing the father could do to keep his heir out was to take the younger son's homage. In principle the son would then have to do the service attributable to that much land, so that as a gift this would become thinkable only as service ceased to be central. But in the late twelfth century it was becoming not only thinkable but common, and bad things happened in consequence. The father of our story makes such a gift to his second son; then the father dies and the eldest succeeds to the inheritance and so becomes the lord of whom the second son holds; and then the second son dies childless. The gift has now lost its purpose, and if homage had not been done the land would have come back to the eldest son and so rejoined the central inheritance as the father would certainly have wished. But as lord of the tenure the eldest son is prevented by the homage from taking the land back if there is anyone who can be heir to the second son. So the land will go to the third son and remain indefinitely a kind of satellite to the family inheritance.[21]

The integrity of the inheritance was important. The father of our story did not want this result and was probably indignant when his lawyer told him it was the only alternative to leaving a younger son at the heir's mercy. One can imagine him asking why so, when he could without risk of such disaster provide for his bastard son.[22] Perhaps it was such a tirade that set the lawyer thinking. The gift to the bastard was innocuous for a reason we have seen: he could have no heirs except his own legitimate is-sue—in the language of the time heirs of himself or heirs of his body. So if he died childless the land would come back to the donor or his heir, rejoining the father's inheritance as the father would want. And the lawyer had a beautiful thought: for the ad hoc purpose of this gift the father would make his legitimate younger son a counterfeit bastard, granting the land to him and the heirs of his body. The aim was only to ensure that the land came back if the grantee died without issue. No grant was yet seen as passing a title which would last beyond the grantee's lifetime, and nobody contemplated that this grant would create an everlasting entail restricted to lineal heirs. But that is what automation ended by doing: the land was programmed into an indefinite future by the words "heirs of his body."

The transformation of essentially managerial arrangements into fixed rights of property produced a very early difficulty of another kind. Suppose a manor with free tenants. Together with his tenement each tenant was entitled to pasture his beasts on the arable land when it was not growing crops, and also on the "wastes" of the manor, those areas mostly on the outskirts of the unit not under cultivation. Seen from the manor court, these wastes were just the environment, and there was no problem about a managerial resolution to develop a particular area by bringing it under cultivation. But when the king's court takes control from the outside there can be no managerial discretion, only fixed rights. Somebody must be seised of the wastes, and it can only be the lord who had been granted the entire unit by the superior lord. But the tenants' rights of pasture must also be something of which they were seised and might be disseised, and must extend over all the areas concerned. The smallest free tenant could therefore stop the greatest lord from developing any of the largest lands. Even if there was ample pasture for him elsewhere in the wastes, he had a right for his beasts to graze on the area chosen for development, and it was protected by a new royal remedy (to be discussed in the following essay) for disseisin. We now know quite a lot about the emergence of this difficulty, and can even name the great lord and the obstinate Hampden who probably forced it onto a royal agenda paper.[23] It ended in a legislative solution which had to counterfeit the managerial discretion:

the tenant was not to win his action if there was enough pasture elsewhere.[24] That story, not in itself of the first importance, provides a clear example of the abrupt change from managerial arrangements to fixed property rights—and of the difficulty it could cause: before there was a superior jurisdiction to which a tenant could turn, a resolution of the lord's court to develop would have been conclusive.[25] Second the difficulty was perceived in substantive terms and was so stated in a memorandum probably emanating from the justices who heard the assize in question.[26] And third the legislative cure was in 1236, centuries before any general legislative adjustment of substantive rights in the area of obligations.[27] The convolutions considered in the preceding essay came about at least partly because in that area direct substantive adjustment was not conceivable. You cannot have substantive legislation until the law is perceived in substantive terms, until the processes considered in the first of these essays had worked their way through. But the law about landholding was always perceived in substantive terms. This was the economic structure. Even in the context of managerial decisions within lords' courts the arrangements of life had to be ordered by explicit criteria. And in that context an essentially legislative change for the future might be included in the disposition of a particular case which had shown up a mischief. In 1260, for example, the county court of Chester was so provoked into an order grappling with the mischief addressed thirty years later in the statute *Quia emptores*.[28]

Quia emptores will feature in the following essay, not so much for its own sake as to make a historiographical point; and it would not further the purpose of this essay to parade particular statutes in order to illustrate what is obvious from any legal history book, namely that legislation played a large part in the history of the land law. But it is worth observing that tension between managerial control and fixed rights is a recurrent theme. The settlor who provided for his daughters and younger sons with immediate gifts of entails and the like might live to regret it, like King Lear. He could reserve a life interest for himself, but, however badly his children treated him, he could not alter the arrangements he had made for what would happen after his death. So he found means to do what the feudal structure had precluded, namely dispose of land by will. By granting his land to friends to whom he could leave instructions he regained a measure of managerial control, which was taken away again by the Statute of Uses, and that turned out to enable settlors to do yet more remarkable things not to be considered in the context of these essays. The story continued. In the nineteenth century managerial needs made it necessary to confer upon tenant for life the powers of an absolute owner, transferring his and all other beneficial interests from the land itself to a trust fund seen as for the time being invested in the land. Conversely in our own day an absolute owner may find that while his legal title is normally inviolable his managerial powers and therefore the value of his property are always at the mercy of planning authorities.

The working of legislation illustrates another persistent theme of these essays: the law is a free-enterprise business. Even if the legislator thought through exactly what he wanted to achieve (which may not always have been the case), he could not foresee the circumstances or control the ways in which his provision would actually be brought to bear, and the eventual consequences often had little relation to what had been envisaged. Nobody at the time could have foreseen, let alone desired, the things the Statute of Uses was made to do. The statute *De donis conditionalibus*[29] unquestionably played a part in the development of the entail, but the draftsman would have been astonished and probably horrified by the final outcome. By the late thirteenth century lawyers had learnt to think in terms of a heritable fee (later to be known as the "fee simple"), and the draftsman was concerned with grants in which he saw the passing of that entity as conditional on the birth of issue; and probably he meant only that satisfaction of the condition should pass the fee not to the donee (who now was never to have more than an estate for his life) but directly to the issue. Only later was he understood to have launched a new kind of cut-down fee restricted indefinitely to lineal heirs, the classical fee tail. The following essay will turn from legal development itself to the ways in which it may be misunderstood by historians, and a chronic misunderstanding is of the scale upon which people were thinking. Legislators and conveyancers did not always (or even often) intend what later times made of their handiwork.

A related misunderstanding goes to the essence of this essay. Historians sometimes say that the difference between custom and law is of small moment, and so it may be if one limits consideration to the immediate outcome of particular facts, to the decision of this present case. By definition custom is very generally followed, and there will be little if any difference in regularity of result. The eldest son will succeed his father in the land whether it is by the lord's court making a customary choice or the king's court applying a legal rule.[30] But even in the context of an immediate inheritance there is a huge difference of perception. When there was only the lord's court, however compelling the customs and the force flowing from the ancestor's homage, the heir could not feel the land was safely "his" until his own homage had been taken, and when it had been taken he would indeed feel that. Royal jurisdiction alters both propositions. Acceptance by the lord is no longer necessary (or, so long as it was seen as necessary, it could be compelled).[31] But equally it is no longer sufficient, and here the difference goes beyond perceptions. There is no safety now. In lords' courts the canons of inheritance had governed only a present choice: in the king's court they could annul a choice made in the past. Suppose an heir who has just succeeded father who in turn had succeeded grandfather: secure as he may seem, he can still be put out by the king's court at the instance of a stranger showing he is now heir to one who was seised long ago. The past is never done with, and that is why an early legislative task was to fence off its remoter reaches with periods of limitation.

Nor is it only the past that can be affected. Consider once more a grant to one "and the heirs of his body." At a time when no grant was seen as passing more than an estate for life, though with an obligation when that life ended to make a new grant to whomever was then heir, those words were meant only to confine the benefit of that obligation to a lineal heir: if the grantee died without issue, the donor-lord could take back the land. No more was intended or expected. But when "fee" and "inheritance" came to be seen not in the customary terms of a new grant for another life but in the legal terms of some ownership descending, the words "and the heirs of his body" were seen as creating the "fee tail," a new cut-down ownership inalienably descending to lineal heirs into an indefinite future.

Custom guided only present decisions. A present decision could of course, as we have seen in connection with the remainder,[32] include a statement of intent about a future decision; but we mislead ourselves if we interpret such arrangements as being of the same nature as the abstract "estates" and "future interests" of the later law. The point can best be made in terms of the early *maritagium*. It has always been discussed as though it was a self-standing entity like the later fee tail, differing mainly in having a fixed expiry date. In fact it was the product of customs about the doing and taking of homage. Homage was not done for maritagium because it would import a duty to do the service, destroy the provisional character of the family "allowance," and attract the "lord-and-heir" consequences. So the woman and her near heirs needed other protection against the donor's heir and got it from two sources, the internal custom of the heir's own court and the external sanction of the church. But this was not an automated entity programmed to end on the entry of the woman's third heir. If that heir was unwilling to do homage (and therewith service), there was just nothing to stop the donor's heir taking the land back. And the early evidence is that heirs before the third might seek to secure themselves by doing homage: it was just that the third could insist.[33] The early maritagium continued or did not continue because of decisions taken on each death; and this is far from the automated devolution of the later fee tail, an "estate" with fixed properties from which (so long as lineal heirs continued) the land could be freed only by extraordinary convolutions.[34] Such abstract constructions were beyond the reach of custom.

IV

HISTORY AND
LOST ASSUMPTIONS

THE PRECEDING ESSAYS HAVE CONSIDERED THE mechanisms by which law first comes into being and then changes. This one will discuss the difficulty of discerning both processes. They cannot easily be seen by historians today largely because they could not be seen to be happening at the time and left no explicit documentary evidence. It is always possible for a visible mischief to be addressed as such by an equally visible process of legislation: but visible mischiefs rarely grow in a customary system, and until the nineteenth century legislation played a small part in private law other than property law. At any one time the law represents a substantial part of the assumptions of society, for which until almost our own day large intentional change is literally unthinkable. But change somehow happens.

Fundamental change happens slowly and by stages so small that nobody at the time could see them as in any way important, let alone as steps toward an unimaginable future. For that reason the orthodoxy of the last half-century by which most kinds of historian project essentially still and close-up pictures, assembling all the evidence for narrow subjects in short periods, is inimical to comprehending the largest legal developments.[1] It is not just that fundamental changes are slow: their visible surface effects may be too widely scattered in subject matter as well as in time for the causation to be demonstrable from particular pieces of evidence. Various of the mischiefs addressed by the outpouring of legislation under Edward I, for example, appear to have followed from changes made under Henry II.[2] As in the natural sciences, fundamental propositions in legal history may stand or fall not with single facts but with their power to explain all the facts.

Perhaps it is only a restatement of that last proposition to say that legal history, more than most kinds of history, depends upon the assumptions with which the materials are read. People do not formulate their assumptions for themselves, let alone spell them out for the benefit of future historians, and in the case of the law there is never occasion to write down what everybody knows.[3] And when everybody has forgotten what everybody once knew, when the assumptions are beyond recall, there is nothing to put the historian on his guard. Not knowing (or even missing) the assumptions of the time, he will read the materials in the light of his own assumptions or those of his predecessors in the field; and, when he or his predecessors have established a framework for one period, that framework will almost inevitably be assumed to be valid for earlier times. Nearly every story considered in this essay will provide an example.

A mistake the historian can easily make is to assume that a blank in his evidence means nothing was happening;[4] and when the materials do begin to show something happening he interprets that as a large change, for which he sometimes imagines large intentions. The history of the common law affords many examples of this phenomenon, so that what was actually slow incremental change is represented as a sporadic series of innovative leaps forward, sudden upsurges of sense or civilization. For the sake of clarity a striking example of this misunderstanding was passed over when the first of these essays described the three modes of proof by which early criminal charges might be determined.[5] If the victim (or in case of homicide his kin) had seen the wrong, he could not only make the accusation but also as witness prove his affirmative oath by battle in what became known as the "appeal of felony." If there was no witness, neighborhood suspicion alone was enough to put a defendant to his oath of denial, but the means by which that oath was tested would depend on what we should call corroboration. If for example there was a corpse or a wound, the oath would be tested by ordeal: but if there was no more than the suspicion of the neighborhood, the oath of denial would be tested by the "lesser law" of compurgation.[6] This last was changed by a legislative act of Henry II: now any accusation of this kind would put the suspect to ordeal or later (after the Church withdrew its sanction from ordeals), to trial by jury.

That was the important change actually made, and to contemporaries it was large enough: there is even reason to think that some disapproved in principle.[7] But it is tiny in comparison to the change imagined by historians until some sixty years ago.[8] They assumed that neighborhood suspicion had previously played no formal part, that the only mode of prosecution had been the "appeal of felony," depending on the victim's initiative and willingness to do battle, and that what the legislation did was to impose an entirely new public duty to "indict" suspects. It is not the only respect in which King Henry II has been credited with instant social engineering on a superhuman scale.

Another story outlined in the first of these essays provides a more insidious example of a blank in the evidence being taken to show that nothing was happening. Legal historians saw the field of what we call tort as divided between essentially separate actions, "trespass *vi et armis*," characterized by direct forcible injury, and "case." Writs in actions on the case were commonly explicit in attributing some fault to the defendant, alleging for example that he had acted negligently. There were no such allegations in trespass, and this predisposed legal historians to conclude that in trespass liability was for centuries strict and fault irrelevant. This conclusion was fortified by another blank: records and reports did not show defendants saying "I was the man, but it was an accident."[9] Apart from stray oddities, discussions of fault in such cases do not appear in reports until the seventeenth century, and their appearance then was seen as another dawn of civilization: reason and decency had broken into a previously barbarous world.

There was much learned discussion on this basis. One scholar, for example, rightly uneasy about supposing there had ever been strict or absolute liability for accidental harm, and rightly suspecting there was something wrong with the question, tried to get rid of it by asserting that all early *vi et armis* actions were for deliberate wrongs. But he was a pure historian, not at his best when thinking through a lawsuit, and it did not occur to him to ask who would tell the victim of an accident that he must not sue. You can always sue, and when the accident victim sued there was nothing the defendant could do but plead Not Guilty, a plea which the same historian assumed to mean only "I was not the man." He went on to adopt an earlier suggestion about the sudden appearance in the seventeenth century of discussions of fault: what had raised the question was the introduction of firearms, which made it possible for an otherwise trivial fault to cause great harm.[10] There had of course always been other dangerous things which might unexpectedly "go off," namely fire and animals, but for these there had been special actions on the case alleging fault.

This and other explanations were unreal because the problem was unreal. The blank had been in the evidence, not in what actually happened. The only change was that discussions of fault, previously sealed up with Not Guilty in the jury room, moved out into a forum where they could be reported and therefore into the vision of historians. The first of these essays sought to explain how in criminal cases juries had to decide for themselves whether a defendant who had killed by accident should be found Guilty or Not Guilty and how the unreported guidelines offered in judges' directions took shape in unreported discussions in the Inns long before procedural change allowed them to be declared in reported judgments.[11]

In civil cases procedural change operated earlier. Under the *nisi prius* system verdicts were taken by delegation in the country and referred back to the court in Westminster, which would normally give judgment accordingly. Mechanisms grew up, however, enabling the party which had lost the verdict to ask the court to do something else instead.[12] The motion for a new trial, to take the relevant example, enabled him to argue that the verdict was unsafe because given on the basis of a misdirection by the trial judge. So principles of liability with which juries had wrestled for centuries, at first with little help from judges and then with help that left no trace for historians, might now be set out in a reported judgment ruling on the propriety of an actual direction. The only novelty was that an old everyday question was for the first time being discussed in the hearing of historians.

It was another seeming blank in the evidence that had conjured up the legal historians' vision of "trespass" and "case" as from the beginning separate entities. There was plenty of "trespass" in the early materials of the common law but just a blank where "case" would later appear, so historians thought nothing relevant was happening in that area. Clarity will be served, however, if what seems to be the true story is told first and the misunderstanding specified later. The second of these essays considered the part played in the development of tort law by allegations of breach of the king's peace.[13] A serious offense against the king requiring royal justice slowly became a label which plaintiffs or their advisers might affix to their lawsuit with no larger intention than obtaining procedural advantage: perhaps they wanted royal rather than local jurisdiction, perhaps jury trial rather than wager of law, perhaps even just process by arrest. What made that slow change possible was that defendants had no way of isolating this allegation for targeted denial. They could only deny generally, and the jurors would give their verdict on the merits without worrying about what appeared to them a technicality.[14]

The only effective limit on manipulation by the plaintiff was formal rather than factual, as can best be seen in terms of the blacksmith and his customer. It was contradictory in itself for the customer to say he had handed his horse over to the defendant smith to shoe and the smith had then injured it against the king's peace.[15] So either the customer must bring an honest action for professional negligence against the smith in a local court, with no mention of the king's peace, and the smith will probably answer by wager of law. Or, if the customer desires some consequence of alleging breach of the king's peace, he must suppress the relationship and sue as he would against a stranger who out of the blue had injured his horse. Since the visible result of his doing so was royal jurisdiction, the historian may (and this one did) conclude that royal jurisdiction was what the customer desired; and it is easy to forget that the evidence would look the same if his real desire had been, for example, to oust the defendant from wager of law, with royal jurisdiction being no more than an acceptable side effect.

That was the situation early in the fourteenth century, and an intentional change was then made, but except to the hindsight of legal historians it was not a large change.[16] An administrative decision was taken, probably in the Chancery, to make writs for wrongs returnable in royal courts without mention of the king's peace. So the customer could now sue the smith for incompetent workmanship in a royal court as openly as he had done in local courts, and without making the wrong look the same as an attack on the horse by a stranger. What is more, claims could also come to royal courts which it had not been possible to dress up as breaches of the king's peace, for example that of the buyer of a defective horse which the seller had asserted to be sound.[17] Claims of both these kinds begin to appear in the records and reports of royal courts in the second half of the fourteenth century. But even in the records numbers are not large, and in the reports there is no suggestion that these were exciting innovations, as of course they were not.

That, however, is not how legal historians saw the matter. Concentrating on materials from royal courts, they took these newly appearing claims to be innovations in real life, remedies for new or previously irremediable wrongs. It is almost as though Englishmen had climbed down from the trees not long before and contented themselves with beating each other up and taking things, and only later had an onset of sophistication suggested subtler kinds of harm. But to explain the perception of historians it is necessary to bring more history to bear. As always in the law, it is largely a matter of words. The reality was that *trespasses* were just wrongs, and that only wrongs said to be in breach of the king's peace could at first be sued on in the king's courts. When other kinds of wrong came to be admitted, writs had to be specially composed, and they were known as writs of "trespass on the case." Over the years and centuries "trespass" and "case"

came to be seen as separate entities, and in the eighteenth century a formal distinction was announced (disastrously, but that is
not our concern)[18]: the characteristic of trespass "against the
king's peace" was declared to be direct forcible injury.

Trespass in that sense was then assumed by historians to have
been the original entity, raising a question about its own origin
and leaving case (or trespass on the case) as a separate entity for
which it was also necessary to find an origin. Everybody imagined
that case evolved by analogy from the supposed primeval direct-
forcible-injury trespass, but how? Was it the exercise of an express power to proceed by analogy conferred upon the Chancery
clerks by a statutory provision of 1285?[19] Or was that statute just
the limited restoration of an inherent power in the Chancery to
create new writs which an earlier provision had taken away? Or
was the statute entirely irrelevant, so that the extension by analogy was by fiat of the judges?[20] There were many learned articles,
and, since most claims in contract and tort came to be made in
actions on the case, the question seemed important. It can now be
seen as unreal because asked on the basis of anachronistic assumptions. But it is in the nature of assumptions that there is no
evidence for them—and they would not be made if there was obvious evidence against them. They just seem to fit.

The assumption that trespass had always been an entity distinguished by direct forcible injury seemed to fit records and reports in which everything called trespass was accompanied by allegations of force and arms and breach of the king's peace. And
when it was suggested (at the time a great heresy) that this association was a result not of substance but of jurisdiction, that a
trespass was just any wrong, but only wrongs in which the king
had an interest could come to his courts, direct evidence for that
proposition was not easy to find. One was driven to scraps like
a statute of 1278 reaffirming that "trespasses" were primarily to

be dealt with in county courts[21] and a very small number of actions in royal courts called "trespass" in which breach of the king's peace was not alleged.[22] So the proposition did not arise from particular pieces of evidence. Particular pieces of evidence were sought for a proposition which was essentially self-evident, either obvious or wrong. The first reaction among legal historians was that it was wrong, the second (many years later) that it was obvious. But the change of mind was still not compelled by specific evidence. The new view just came to be accepted as the better fit, providing a single satisfactory explanation of the evidence as a whole.

What camouflaged this entire development was the changing meaning of a word. In reading the thirteenth- and early fourteenth-century materials, legal historians did not invent the direct-forcible-injury sense of *trespass*: they carried it back from a later time. And since it is in the connotations of key words that legal assumptions reside, they carried the later assumptions back with it. The damage to the intellectual history of the law went far beyond the endless theories about "origins" prompted by the artificially narrowed sense of *trespass*. The loss of its natural broad sense caused historians to misunderstand the terms in which lawyers were thinking, especially in the fourteenth and fifteenth centuries. Instead of simple concepts of the order of "tort" and "contract," *trespass* and *covenant* were understood as mere "forms of action," in which category they were joined by another, namely *case;* and elementary legal argument was mistaken for an almost Darwinian struggle[23] in which these mysterious entities jostled for survival.[24]

That mechanistic vision is another example of the assumptions of a later period carried back into an earlier.[25] The assumptions wrongly imposed upon the fourteenth and fifteenth centuries were truly those of the seventeenth and eighteenth, when

lawyers were indeed arguing in terms not of elementary categories of claim but of the boundaries between actions, including
most remarkably the boundary between "trespass" and "case."[26]
The narrowed sense of *trespass* must have been the main cause of
this change,[27] but the second of these essays suggested that the artificialities there considered may have played a part. To allow an
action on the case on facts for which (say) debt was appropriate
was a less uncomfortable impropriety than expressly to remedy a
contractual complaint by giving the "wrong" damages in a tort
action.[28] In the nineteenth century the distinctive properties of the
separate actions were abolished, though in a piecemeal way;[29]
and it is no coincidence that as abolition of the "forms of action"
proceeded lawyers once more began to think in terms of elementary categories, now called "tort" and "contract." But even then
they could not do without "trespass" which had to live on as "a"
tort. What started as a broad elementary category ends as a narrow and highly artificial entity, a name which imports many rules
of law.

In turning to another word, one for which a jurisdictional
change had even more profound consequences, the writer suffers
a continuing embarrassment. His suggestion about the original
sense of *trespass* was long rejected as heresy before suddenly being taken to be obvious. But an equally obvious suggestion about
the original sense of *seisin* is still condemned as heresy by many
medievalists, for whom more is at stake. Carrying back the later
narrow sense of *trespass* did considerable damage, but only to the
internal intellectual history of the law. With *seisin* reconsideration of the original sense would entail reconsideration of other or-
thodoxies in medieval history.

There is another difference. The later sense of *trespass* was
carried back unconsciously, assumed without discussion. But
seisin has provoked much discussion in the last hundred years,[30]

and the assumption of historians has played a rather different part. There was no clear-cut later sense that could be carried back, but there was a clear-cut analogy. Historians have assumed that seisin was always an abstract relationship between a person and a thing of the same nature as possession and have therefore focused discussion on situations in which one who plainly had possession, especially the leaseholder,[31] could not be said to have seisin. For us that is perhaps the most obtrusive of the puzzles raised by the assumption, certainly the easiest to grasp; but it is almost insignificant compared with the anomalies raised by viewing the classical common law of property in the light of the same assumption.

Those anomalies, never really known to historians and now all but forgotten even among lawyers, were most strikingly brought out by Maitland in two articles written before his *History of English Law* was conceived, and he accepted that they arose from his own equations (from which he never wavered) of seisin with possession and the right with ownership.[32] In his article on "The Mystery of Seisin" he writes:

> The owner who is not seised . . . seems hardly to have ownership . . . because as regards such matters as the alienation, transmission, devolution of his rights he seems to be in a quite different position from that in which we should expect to find a person who, though he has not possession, has yet ownership.[33]

His detailed exposition cannot be bettered, but it may be useful to repeat the two main propositions, both of which remained law into the nineteenth century. However much right a man had, he could not grant it away unless he was in seisin; so the right in itself was inalienable. And unless one with the right had himself also been in seisin, nobody could ever claim it as his heir: "a very remarkable rule," wrote Maitland, "for it comes to this . . . that ownership is not inheritable."[34]

If the characteristics which ownership conjures up for us, especially alienability and heritability, were associated more nearly with seisin, what is left as the content of "the right"? In the thirteenth century it is nothing more than the ability to bring a "writ of right" claiming seisin from the person who now has seisin: and in that action the only case the claimant can make is as heir of one who was seised.[35] If his father acquired it five years ago from a family who had had it for centuries, he must base his claim on the seisin of his father and cannot even mention the ancestral holding of his father's grantors. It is an odd form of ownership, very odd indeed if one thinks in Maitland's terms (explicitly carried back from his own day) of ownership as deriving from the oldest seisin.[36]

Artificiality took further turns. Claims ceased to be brought to the lord's court by writ of right, and later the claimant did not generally begin in a court at all. He just went into the land expecting to be ejected by the person in seisin, which might have been long and peaceful. This enabled him (and here the reader may need to suspend disbelief) to bring the most summary of royal remedies, the assize of novel disseisin, on the basis that by going in with something known as a "right of entry" the claimant had himself instantly become seised and was therefore disseised by the ejection. Later still the framework of litigation became even more artificial, but rights of entry continued to be the basis of most claims, and only exceptionally was a claimant driven to the old kind of action based directly on "the right." This was the main topic (though not the avowed subject) of Maitland's article on "The Beatitude of Seisin,"[37] and it makes seisin an odd form of possession, and the assize of novel disseisin an extremely odd form of possessory protection.

The proposition that seisin was always a variant of possession is intertwined with the belief that the assize of novel disseisin was introduced as possessory protection of the Roman kind and perhaps consciously on the Roman model. The essence of such protection is that the victim of a taking can recover from the taker without having to prove any title beyond his possession. Previously, on this view, the only action for the recovery of land had been the writ of right claiming "ownership."[38] That action had to be brought in the court of the lord of whom the land was claimed to be held, and was cumbersome. In novel disseisin Henry II and his advisers provided a quicker and more convenient remedy for persons dispossessed, and because it was only "possessory" (the key element in this theory) it did not trench upon the monopoly jurisdiction of feudal lords over "proprietary" actions in "the right." What is more, it was the spearhead of a range of possessory remedies, culminating in the "writs of entry," which by their greater efficiency were to attract all disputes into the king's courts and make the writ of right all but obsolete; and many historians have supposed that this monopolization was the object aimed at from the beginning.[39]

Without the backing of Maitland's authority, it would take an unalterable faith in coincidence still to see generalized protection of abstract possession as the aim of the novel disseisin writ. Its very specific wording at every point appears precisely tailored to an equally specific mischief, namely abuse of a humdrum seignorial routine which Maitland never mentioned and of which he may not have been conscious. That routine was preeminent among those everyday things which disappear almost without trace, the kind of lost assumption central to this essay. The tenant in seisin was not "owner," but he had tenure in the sense in which the professor or the judge has tenure; and if he defaulted on his service or the like he could in the last resort be deprived, but only by that due process of his lord's court which was briefly described in the third of these essays.[40]

A series of summonses was followed by a series of distraints by chattels, and only after that might the court make any order affecting the land. The writ of novel disseisin requires the chattels to be put back, a unique requirement and uniquely appropriate to a process in which distress by chattels had to come before any taking of the land. If the defendant could not be found, his bailiff was to be summoned; so the defendant aimed at by the draftsman was at least somebody's lord, presumably the plaintiff's.[41] And the disseisin was said to have been done "unjustly and without judgment," which Maitland explained as aimed against self-help in the assertion of genuine claims which should have been made by legal action[42]—exactly what came to happen with "rights of entry." Nor can the congruity between the words of the writ and the enforcement routine itself be dismissed as coincidence: our detailed knowledge of the routine actually comes from early plea roll entries in which the defendant is a lord resisting novel disseisin on the basis that he acted by due process of his court, of which he has to give a step-by-step account.[43]

The equation of seisin with possession brought with it separate anomalies, and separate explanations were provided. The leaseholder's lack of seisin was attributed by Maitland to a Roman analogy,[44] but has since attracted other suggestions. Rights of entry were said to flow from a statement in *Bracton* that one disseised had four days for self-help before the disseisor himself became protected by the assize.[45] But if that is so the days became decades, and the initial event giving rise to the right of entry must always have amounted to a disseisin. The greatest anomaly, the association with seisin rather than with the right of nearly all the properties one would expect of ownership, was explained by Maitland as the legacy of a society which could not conceive of rights over things as existing apart from the things themselves: "old impotencies of mind give rise to rules which perdure long after they have ceased to be the only conceivable rules."[46] No historian of English law could deny that it is a medium in which things perdure, especially words and forms of words; but this one at least is always troubled by explanations depending upon "old impotencies of mind."[47]

There is a more fundamental consequence, and not only for legal historians, of seeing seisin and the right as abstract entities of the nature of the modern possession and ownership. The vision assumes an essentially modern social and economic structure. Land is just property as in modern England or ancient Rome. A unitary law supports rights which exist in the abstract, and its concepts and rules are outside and above the courts which apply them. Those courts are purely judicial bodies which have no managerial function and which, at any rate in civil matters, apply those external rules to settle disputes between legal equals. "Ownership" leaves no room for a tenure like that of the professor or the judge, or for that due process by which a tenant's duties to his lord were enforced by the judgment of his peer tenants. This was the routine business of lords' courts: but that due process, central to the assumptions of the time, was emasculated by the working of novel disseisin and left as direct evidence only a handful of cases in the earliest plea rolls for historians to overlook.[48]

Things look different if you do not assume a modern world, if there was no unitary law existing in the sky but just the more or less uniform customs of separate lords' courts in actual control. By definition those customs were very generally followed, but in any particular case what the court in fact did was final. In the preceding essay we considered the nature of "the right" in such a world: just a claim to be admitted as heir when the ancestor has died; and if despite the custom the claim is passed over, whether by malice or mistake, the heir has no redress until there is a superior jurisdiction to which he can turn. And when royal jurisdiction established regular control with its "writ of right," we saw how "the right" suddenly changed into a kind of ownership.[49]

How does seisin look in that same world? It looks like possession in the most obvious physical sense, and a tenant of the twelfth century, however knowledgeable, might not have given much of an answer if asked to spell out the difference between his seisin and a Roman possession. What he would have seen was the practical essence of both: actually having the land or other thing (and that is why he would not have thought it anomalous to speak of the seisin of chattels).[50] What he would not have seen, because unable to step outside his own mind and reckon with his own assumptions, was the difference in jurisdictional context: seisin of his tenement depended upon his lord's authority and nobody could be seised without that authority. Within the closed world of the lord's court any seisin was by definition rightful.[51] Antithesis between seisin and right came when the tenant in seisin in his lord's court could be ousted by the superior jurisdiction of the king's court. And finally, when the lord's court faded away and there was only the one open world of the king's court, an English seisin like a Roman possession could be wrongful as well as rightful.

But if seisin in an obvious factual way looks like possession, there is also an important sense in which it looks like ownership: it is the most you can have. The tenant in seisin has tenure. Subject to the possibility of being deprived by the due process of his lord's court for failure of service or the like (and it was to protect him against improper deprivation that the assize of novel disseisin was originally introduced), the tenant has all he can have, namely full enjoyment of the land, for all the time he can have, namely his lifetime. When that life ends the lord must, as it were, hire a new man. He will make a new grant to a new tenant, and the custom of his court and the almost sacramental force of homage will constrain him to make it to the dead tenant's heir—and the cycle will begin again. But cycle it is. There are successive seisins, but no ownership to descend through the generations and no mystery about the attachment to seisin of the properties which a modern lawyer would associate with ownership.

Each tenant in that cycle was seised by the lord, and the verb brings out a point which *seisin* as a noun hides. If tenant for life is in seisin but tenant for years is not, though he is in possession, there is evidently a difference in sense between the two nouns, but at least they work in the same way. The verbs do not. "I possess my book" is a proposition involving no other person—or every other person in the world. But a tenant could not say "I seise my land": he could not be the nominative subject or the land the accusative object. The land had to go into the genitive, the tenant was the object, and you needed another person as the subject: the lord seised the tenant of the land. The connotations are those of a relationship between two persons about the thing, not just an abstract relationship between the thing and one person.

It is the verb in the active mood that requires a subject: the passive is more accommodating. And it is no coincidence that while the sources go on describing people as seised of their land, they cease to speak of one person seising another. Instead they resort to the equally accommodating noun: the one person "makes" or "delivers" seisin to the other. The connotations of relationship between two persons are being lost, and the change in linguistic usage reflects a change in actuality. It had been a lord who seised a tenant and who might disseise him, and so long as he and his court were in control seisin was not abstract possession in an open world: it was tenured possession by his authority—the only authority that was relevant. But the world changed after the king provided the assize of novel disseisin for tenants who had been disseised wrongly, that is put out by or on the authority of the lord but without due process of his court. This provided almost summary recovery of the land, and it came to be used against others than the lord. And since other royal remedies also produced the result that one could be seised by the king's order but without the lord's acceptance, the word lost its original connotations. It became abstract, a sort of possession, precisely because it was now being used in a unitary society ruled by the single law of the king's court.

So it was the superimposition of royal jurisdiction that turned seisin into a kind of abstract possession. And in a remarkable passage Maitland himself for a moment saw this, observing not only that the original concept of seisin must have been relative to the court of the lord concerned but also that this relativity must have been destroyed by Henry II's provision of direct royal protection.[52] But it was a fleeting insight he never followed up, and elsewhere he had expressly rejected the idea that seisin originally involved at least the lord's acquiescence.[53] He thought there was no evidence for that, and indeed there is not much direct and explicit evidence. But then there never is direct and explicit evidence for assumptions. It would not have occurred to anybody at the time to examine the connotations of *seisin* any more than it occurred to anybody at the time to ask why the leaseholder was not seised. Within the framework of their world those things went without saying and without analysis.

How far could anybody at the time have seen these changes as they happened? The direct effect of royal jurisdiction was certainly visible. A chronicler thought it worth noting that in 1192 the abbot of Bury St. Edmunds would not summarily disseise defaulting tenants, for the expressed reason that it would place him in the king's mercy "by assise of the realm."[54] The extension of the assize to remedy other dispossessions is something about which we may never learn much. Though we have plea rolls from 1194, entries hardly ever set out the facts or show the relationship of the parties. There is just a blank general verdict. But defendants are sometimes identified as manorial officers, and sometimes without the lord being joined;[55] so it is easy to imagine the stages by which plaintiffs came to widen the use made of the assize.

And about this, and every other extension of an action beyond its original purpose, it is important to remember the free-enterprise quality of the legal world. The legislator of course had a specific mischief in mind when he prescribed his remedy, but he had no control once it was launched. There was nobody to monitor the use made of his creature, nobody able to veto an "improper" application.[56] There was no propriety. The plaintiff did not have to worry whether he would be allowed this writ which might give him such rapid redress, only whether if he got it the twelve men would answer in his favor the question put to them.

Even if, as is likely, the extension of the assize happened quickly enough to be visible to contemporaries, it is unlikely in the extreme that anybody ever noticed the concomitant change in the connotations of *seisin*. The word just went on being used within a changing framework, and English lawyers, unconcerned with the past, worked within the framework of their day on the questions of their day. The "mystery" and the "beatitude" were largely of Maitland's own making when he forced on an earlier time concepts of ownership and possession at home in his own (or a Roman) world, a world in which a piece of land is not held in return for service and other obligations and so is not in any meaningful sense a tenement: it is just a piece of freestanding property, something that can be taken without consequence for anyone except the taker and his victim.

But little if any of this is susceptible of proof by the deployment of particular pieces of evidence. Changing assumptions do not leave particular pieces of evidence, only incremental changes of behavior which may result in small adjustments scattered over wide areas of the law and over long periods of time: but the causation can hardly be proved, only inferred. Consider for example what hindsight (but only hindsight) can see as the long-term consequences of the assize of novel disseisin on the process it was intended to regulate, that due process of lords' courts for the enforcement of services. The blankness of most enrolments makes it hard to be sure, but the early plea rolls suggest that lords generally kept out of trouble by stopping short of the last stage of that process and not touching the land itself. In all ordinary cases distress by chattels would do the job. But it was no good against the tenant who in effect abandoned his tenement and left it without chattels which might be distrained. Is it coincidence that, nearly a century after Henry II died, statute[57] should have dealt with that mischief by providing an action which enabled the lord to do in the king's court what he would once have done in his own, namely get back the tenement?

That story may be taken further. If the lord steered clear of novel disseisin by not touching the land, and provided he kept within the jurisdictional boundaries of his fee, he largely steered clear of royal control of his enforcement procedure.[58] Partly for that reason, and partly because subinfeudations had produced many "lords" who had tenants owing service but did not have courts, distress by chattels became an independent remedy which a lord could use without any judgment of his court; and the tenant, who would previously have replevied any distress in that court, was driven to public justice in the county court.[59] A bizarre possibility followed. When a lord "avowed" his taking as distress for services in arrear, the tenant could with impunity deny owing him any service. This amounted to a denial that he held any land of the lord, and on that basis the lord was amerced for distraining out of his fee.

The extent of this mischief has been questioned.[60] But it could happen, and its enormity shows a background in which the tenant's "disclaimer" would have been unthinkable, an automatic forfeiture of the tenement. If it had been on record, as it would be if the lord instead of distraining had sought to recover his services by action in the king's court, the lord could recover the land by "writ of right on disclaimer."[61] But the county was not a court of record, and legislation, again of 1285,[62] permitted a lord to have the replevin proceedings removed from the county to the king's court where a disclaimer would be fatal. Hindsight can see the whole structure, including the shadowy "writ of right on disclaimer" as a patchwork of expedients, and the holes to be patched as all caused by the disintegration of that unitary enforcement process of lords' own courts. They would have ordered the distress in the first place, have themselves heard the replevin proceedings, and have themselves (on their own authority without royal writ) adjudged a forfeiture for the feudal felony of denying the tenure.[63]

Again, however, none of this can be demonstrated in a way which would satisfy most historians of the present generation, even if they could bring themselves to consider together events as far apart as 1166 and 1285. The hindsight is of connections which could hardly have been seen even at the time. The tenant disclaiming in the county court meant to take advantage of what he probably saw as a lucky loophole in the framework of his day, and the legislator meant to close it; but probably neither knew how the loophole had arisen. Similarly the legislator, having to deal with tenements abandoned without chattels which might be distrained, was just solving a present problem, and he may have had no idea that in providing the lord with an action in the king's court to get the land back he was counterfeiting the ultimate power that lords had once exercised on their own authority in their own courts.

So, as with the sense of *trespass*, the "feudal" sense of *seisin* is something else that is either obvious or wrong; and the only realistic test is whether this or the "possessory" sense provides the more satisfactory explanation of all the facts and all the oddities. Of the greatest oddity, the association with seisin rather than with the right of the properties which we associate with ownership rather than with possession, no more need be said. The rules that perdured did not flow from the impotencies of mind invoked by Maitland[64] but from the assumptions of an essentially sovereign lordship in which any seisin was rightful in the sense that it carried the lord's authority, a tenement was in principle the price of a man's service, and tenure for his life was the most the man could have.

As his lord's man it was also the least he could have. The term of years was simply not within this framework of thought, but just one of the ways in which the man might exploit his tenement. He could manage it himself, or appoint a bailiff to manage it and (he hoped) yield up the actual profits, or he could "sell" the actual profits for a period by a contract farming them out to a termor, who would keep them as part of some loan arrangement or pay him a fixed rent. None of these things affected the relationship between lord and man. If for example the man died leaving an infant heir the lord was not limited to taking rent as he would be limited to the service of a grantee by subinfeudation. He disregarded the term of years and took the tenement in wardship, the contract between man and termor was suspended, and the unexpired term of years would begin to run again when the heir came of age.[65] Our question has arisen not from the realities of the time but from our own assumption of a range of "estates in land." It is not only that the leasehold came to be upgraded from a contractual arrangement about the profits into a bastard tenure of the land. The life interest itself was downgraded by the idea of ownership: from being the most a man could have it became something limited. And so, as with the widow's dower and the widower's curtesy,[66] things look alike to us which in the framework of their time were not even comparable.

The remaining oddity is the right of entry. It may not now be possible to make sense even of the later learning, so copious and intricate did it become. And early details may be equally irretrievable, lost (with much else) behind the normally blank enrollments of assizes of novel disseisin. Without a time machine we shall never normally be able to hear what was said in any actual assize that ended in the almost invariable general verdict,[67] but providence led a writer of about 1240 to include a made-up example in a tract using made-up examples to explain what happened in various kinds of court.[68] The plaintiff says just that he was in peaceful seisin, without explaining how he came to be there. The defendant says that his father died seised, and the lord therefore put him in seisin. This was not a formal "exception," a reason for the judges not to take the assize, which in a real case the clerk might have enrolled.[69] It was just an explanation for the twelve men, and the plea roll would have recorded only a general verdict that the defendant had or had not disseised the plaintiff. There would have been no reference to anything the parties had said, and in particular no mention of the lord, although, for the writer of the tract (who was presumably representing typical cases), the lord had been the central figure.

Looking backward in this essay, that imaginary case has obvious relevance to the proposition that assent of the lord was inherent in the original concept of seisin. In that context it may be set beside a real assize of 1222 in which we know the facts because bemused recognitors were allowed to return a special verdict,[70] which told of a prolonged series of takings and retakings between feuding relatives. The court decided that the party who had gone in with the lord's consent had been seised, significantly adding that the other party had no "warrant" for their seisin.[71] The historian of novel disseisin noted cases in which something turned on who had gone in "by" the lord; but, being wedded to the "possessory" view of the assize and to the proposition that rights of entry derived from a time limit for retaking of the nature of *Bracton*'s four days, it did not occur to him that the lord's assent might be the original essence of all rights of entry.[72]

Once again we are up against the lost meaning of a word. *Entry* has been assumed to denote a physical event, just person going into the land. But all the thirteenth-century evidence suggests seignorial connotations: it was not the physical tenement that you entered but the fee of the lord.[73] The outstanding example is the preamble to *Quia emptores*, to be discussed below, in which the mischief of subinfeudation is said to be that purchasers from tenants are "entering the fees" of their lords, who thereby lose wardships and the like.[74]

Again, consider the *praecipe* writs of "entry" which brought claims not to the lord's court but directly to the king's. They recited some defect in an event or transaction essential to the defendant's title, and have traditionally been explained, in defiance even of *Bracton*,[75] as "possessory" remedies descended from novel disseisin.[76] But their development and jurisdictional bearing are more comprehensively explained on the basis that a "lord" (the heir of a grantor by subinfeudation)[77] was questioning the "entry" of one holding as his tenant: this man is not entitled to be my tenant, says a claimant, because he got in by grant from my ancestor who (for example) was out of his mind when he made it.

For such a situation it was proper to bring a *praecipe* writ directly to the king's court (rather than a writ of right to the lord's), not because the claim was "possessory" but because the claimant's lord would any way not have jurisdiction over a defendant who was not his own tenant.[78]

After the ending of subinfeudation by *Quia emptores*, however, the grantee in such a case would indeed have held of the grantor's lord, who would therefore properly have jurisdiction over the claim. But in practice by this time lords' courts were seldom or never handling claims begun by writ of right patent, and in principle all such claims would have been subjected to the old routine of removal to the county and then to the king's court.

What actually happened, as we know, was an increase in more summary litigation depending upon rights of "entry." Perhaps they started as an exercise of what may be described as the lord's nonjudicial authority. His court did not hear a case or give a judgment. He just authorized a claimant to take seisin, and any assize or other lawsuit would involve the claimant and not the lord, as in the real case above of 1222 or the made-up case of about 1240.[79] And then he became formalized, leaving a right of entry as something a lord could have authorized. We come back once more to language. The year books do not speak of "rights" of entry: their phrase is *entre congeable*. If *entry* meant entry into the fee of a lord, and an entry is said to be "*congeable*" or "permissible," the person who could give permission was presumably the lord.

This may explain one of the oddities in the later learning. In its intimidating language the most prominent of the events which might "toll" a right of entry (leaving the claimant with only a right of action) was the "descent cast." If the man now in had come to the land by inheritance, the claimant's right of entry was gone. It is hard to imagine how this could have flowed from logic like that of *Bracton*'s four days. But on the logic of seignorial assent as an ingredient of seisin, this was a case in which the lord had in principle already given his assent—to the heir when he inherited. The diminishing part played by the lord in the mechanics of inheritance is the key. What started as a new grant to the heir was first required by custom and the force of homage, then it was compelled by the king's court, and finally it was assumed. In real life the lord's part was formalized out of existence, leaving inheritance as that mystical autonomous event which lasted until 1897: and we have generally supposed that the formalization came about all at once as a result of the Assize of Northampton in 1176. But the evidence is of a slow process of erosion. In some situations, particularly when there was doubt over who was heir, lords long continued to play a real part. In others the sources show a process of fictionalization. They show also that the one person who became instantly seised (the hallmark of a right of entry) was the heir entering as such.[80]

And this brings us back to the proposition that the right-of-entry mechanism was not confined to retrieving land lost by disseisin. It was a general way of asserting title, and there was no title except that by inheritance. That was the title which we first see a claimant setting up in his lord's court on a writ of right. And we are probably wrong in seeing rights of entry as somehow an innovation. A writ of right had been required when the lord was "against" the claimant, either because he had taken homage from another tenant or because he thought himself entitled to hold on his own account.[81] One exercising a right of entry had the lord actually or (later) supposedly on his side. In principle this was the commonplace situation in which the undisputed heir was put in by the lord or went in with his assent. The extraordinary right of entry and the even more extraordinary common-law vision of inheritance as passing title to the heir with no official authentication can be seen as twin ghosts: lords were still haunting a lord-less world.

So far this essay has been concerned with large differences of interpretation caused by what seem to be wrong assumptions, by the disappearance of things that in their time were obvious and so went without saying, and it may be useful to suggest more particular misunderstandings so caused. Decent shame requires that the first example should be a mistake made by the writer himself. He first expressed doubts about Maitland's analysis of the medieval materials in terms of "ownership and possession" as long ago as 1968, but he was not then sufficiently thoroughgoing in his heresy. Locked into the dogma that the best title was that derived from the oldest seisin,[82] he made a damaging mistake about the factual basis for a claim by writ of right. He assumed that the ancestor from whose seisin the "count" had to begin was the earliest ancestor the claimant knew to have been seised, and this lent continuing color to the idea of a heritable ownership.[83] It was nearly thirty years[84] before it occurred to the writer that problems and mysticism vanish together if the ancestor was the latest of the claimant's ancestors to have been seised (before the land got into the "wrong" hands, as in a writ of entry) so that the pedigree was not tracing a "title" through the generations, just showing that the claimant was now that ancestor's heir.

That misunderstanding was of a whole class of material, namely the counts as represented (in Latin) in plea rolls and (in French) in formularies like *Novae Narrationes*. What is usually affected is the understanding of a single text. A monastic chronicle records a small drama enacted within about thirty years of the Conquest. A military tenant of Abingdon Abbey died leaving an infant son and a greedy brother. The brother first asked to have the land for himself, but when the abbot held (literally) to the boy the brother changed tack and made a new and successful request to have the land for the duration of the infancy, doing the service due. Though the editor's translation makes it as clear as does the Latin text that there were two distinct requests, and that the first was altogether abandoned, his headnote summary represents one single request which was first refused then accepted. To one assuming a hereditary ownership the wardship arrangement sought by the second request was thinkable, but not the request the brother first made—that the infant son should be passed over altogether and the land granted to the brother instead.[85]

Another example concerns *Glanvill*'s treatment of wardship during the infancy of an heir holding of several lords. Under Henry III each lord took wardship of the lands held of himself, and the only special perquisite of the "chief lord" (here meaning the lord of the oldest tenure) was wardship of the heir's person and therewith the marriage. Except for cases in which one of the lords was the king, this pattern remained so long as wardships lasted, and it enshrined the logic that the lord who could not have his service because of the infancy should have the issues of the land instead. And in this, as in so much else, historians have assumed that the pattern had always obtained and have imposed it on *Glanvill*'s account.[86] This imposition, as will appear, attributes improbably sloppy language to that most precise of writers. It also postulates a legal anomaly which either has not been recognized as such or has been accepted in silence, making *Glanvill* assert that the lords get their reliefs and services as well as the wardship. There are express statements that this could not happen,[87] and anyway it does not make sense: if the wardship brought all the revenues to the lord, there was nothing left from which relief and service could separately be provided.

With a single apparent exception every word of *Glanvill*'s account is unambiguously (and with the writer's usual precision) describing a very different arrangement by which any chief lord took wardship of the heir and his entire inheritance, as the king continued to do with his "prerogative wardship."[88] The seemingly dissonant word is a personal pronoun. Wardship of the entirety (*per totum*) is given *eis*; and since the persons last mentioned are the other lords, grammar has been taken to reinforce imposition of the later pattern (even though that involves reversing the translation of *ita quod* from "so that" to "but," depriving *per totum* of any force, and swallowing the impossibility of having wardship, relief, and services together). But the grammatical norm may always be overridden when the pronoun obviously refers not to the person last mentioned but to the subject of the passage as a whole, and a characteristic of legal texts is that their writers were always addressing people who shared their assumptions and knew what and whom they meant. The subject matter of this passage was certainly obvious to those who wrote the rubric in the principal manuscripts: "The wardship of chief lords."[89] It is another example of something obvious being overlaid by the assumptions of a later time.

A more far-reaching example concerns the background to the statute *Quia emptores*, which protected the interests of lords by requiring grants to be by substitution, so that the grantee became tenant of the grantor's lord, rather than subinfeudation, by which the grantee would hold as tenant of the grantor. The assumption has been that lords always had two bundles of rights, on the one hand the regular services, and on the other the occasional "incidents" to which they were entitled on the death of a tenant. Both bundles are seen as always valuable, so that wardships, for example, were always desired: what changed was only their relative value. Except for the relief payable by an adult heir, the incidents brought the issues of the land itself to the lord, for example wardship during an infancy; so these held their real value. The services of a military tenant, by contrast, were converted into money payments which first fell in real value and then ceased to be raised.[90] The financial interest of lords therefore became concentrated upon their incidents, and the standard account of the matter sees the statute as a response to "machinations" by tenants.[91] By subinfeudating in return for a large sum of money (none of which would come to the lord) and reserving as service (which a wardship or escheat would bring to the lord) something nominal like a rose at midsummer, they deprived the lord for ever of the real value of his seignory. So on this view the statute was precipitated by deliberate and recent "tax-avoidance" arrangements.

What really happened was less simple, less calculated, and far less quick. When service was what was desired, the death of a tenant leaving an infant heir was not a bonus for the lord: it was a problem to which we have seen him finding various solutions.[92] He would be actually glad to have that problem permanently obviated by a subinfeudation reserving the service he was owed, which he would then regularly get without having to make special arrangements on every infancy. Such reservation of the "upward" service was general, and as service ceased to be valuable that itself (and not such contrivances as roses at midsummer) is what dwindled into the "nominal service" of the classical account. Correspondingly the money payment, at first in principle a makeweight, grew toward the "market value" of the land. The vision of tricks by estate planners comes from assuming that the seignorial relationship was essentially static. The real cause of the statute was the slow reversal of the economic interests of the parties. This could hardly be seen at the time,[93] let alone by historians confining themselves within the customary periods.

The preeminent example of all the ambiguous understandings considered in this essay (and of the unpredictable quality of legislation mentioned in the last) is provided by the changes made under King Henry II, and particularly the introduction of the assize of novel disseisin. The most visible sequel was that all litigation about freehold land was over time transferred from feudal to royal courts; and we have seen that many historians took this jurisdictional diversion (understood as depending upon the superior competitive attraction of the royal remedies and as exploiting the supposed distinction between possessory and proprietary claims) to have been the object aimed at by calculating legislators.[94]

More fundamentally it has been assumed that the change of jurisdiction was the only important sequel, that the same claims were being made in much the same terms but in different courts, and therefore that what you cannot see going on in lords' courts in the twelfth century must have been been of the same nature as what you can see in the king's courts in the thirteenth. On that basis there must always have been fixed rules and abstract concepts like ownership and possession: but how the rules and abstractions came into existence is a question nobody asked. The answer is yet another thing that is either obvious or wrong: the criteria by which feudal courts ordered their affairs were transformed into instant law by the jurisdictional change itself. The claim of an heir against the dead tenant's lord to be admitted to this present vacancy suddenly became a sort of ownership which can override the decision the lord actually took on a former vacancy.[95] And the seisin of a tenant, by definition rightful in the closed legal world of his lord's court, became an odd kind of possession outside that matrix and in the open world of the king's court.

Nor is this a change only in the elementary concepts of property law. It is a change in the economic and political constitution of society. The real English Revolution was started by a king, and it left lords having economic but not governmental power and being equal with their tenants before the law of the king's courts. The end result was as far beyond the foresight of Henry II as would have been the transfer of jurisdiction which many have supposed that he intended. But if one reads the writ of novel disseisin side by side with the handful of surviving cases in which a defendant lord expressly relies on the due process of his court, one can only conclude that the king meant precisely to hold lords to their own customs of a tenure which could be disturbed or ended only by that due process. The existing framework was to be subjected to a very precise rule of law with external enforcement of the safeguard upon which the tenure of every freehold tenant was seen to be hinged, namely the judgment of his peers.

The thrust of that phrase in *Magna Carta*[96] was plainly to subject the king himself to the same safeguard in relation to his own tenants, but it has been a puzzle almost from the time of the Charter itself. This is partly because the essential hurt could not be stated in isolation: all judgments in local as well as seignorial courts had been by peers whereas the newfangled royal jurisdiction, even when regularly exercised, was entrusted to appointees. But the specific grievance of the barons was action against themselves, particularly disseisins, ordered either by ad hoc bodies or at the king's mere will without any sort of judgment.[97] And the main cause of puzzlement is that the core load-bearing role of the *judicium parium* was itself approaching redundancy and its long oblivion. The plea rolls suggest that by 1215 it was already rare for lords' courts to push their everyday enforcement process beyond distress by chattels, so novel disseisin, designed to protect the tenure of freeholders, was ensuring that it never even came in question. Tenants were turning into landowners, in the end leaving only such as professors and judges to enjoy a meaningful tenure.

The important substantive effect was on the perception of the tenant's position, which lost its most obviously dependent feature.[98] But our immediate concern is the effect on the understanding of the Charter. Except as an aspiration against the one lord never subject to novel disseisin, the lord king, there was now no everyday context in which the judgment of peers conjured up the old security of tenure;[99] and there began a search for the meaning of this phrase by which the Charter had set such store. The least acceptable theory (still sometimes voiced in ill-informed debate) took it as a reference to jury trial. For historians today it seems to represent only an imprecise notion of social equality between judges and judged,[100] and indeed little else remains of this *Hamlet* when its Prince of Denmark is left out. A basic assumption of society has been lost, and with it the thinking of the principal actors in great events—the advisers of King Henry II and to a lesser extent the barons of King John.

It is because law has to present the appearance of continuity that change comes about behind such screens as unchanging words. Things so obvious that they go without saying in their own day simply disappear, and the historian reads his materials in the light of what seems obvious to himself. The important differences between the world he sees and the world he does not see cannot (as it were) be checked off by noting changes of detail in the margins of standard works. This devil is not in the detail but in the framework within which the detail is perceived. That is not something you can set out to look for; and if you stumble upon it, because distracted by incongruities when working within the received framework, you must resign yourself to being a heretic.

NOTES

INTRODUCTION

1. Below, essay 1 at n. 31.
2. F. W. Maitland, introduction to YB 1 and 2 Edward II (17 Selden Society) xvii.
3. F. Pollock and F. W. Maitland, *History of English Law*, 2 vols. (Cambridge, 1898 [1895]). The terminal date excluded discussion of year books, and it is noteworthy that the one examination of a year book case (II:180) did prompt related observations, below, essay 1 at n. 8.
4. End of essay 1.
5. See *Select Canterbury Cases* (95 Selden Society), introduction, 45–52, and "Early Cases (c. 1200)," 1–48.
6. A separate consequence, irrelevant in the present context but still potentially interesting to legal historians, was the representation of some arrangements as licences rather than leases.
7. F. W. Maitland, "Why the History of English Law Is Not Written" (inaugural lecture), *Collected Papers* (Cambridge, 1911), I:480 at 493–94.
8. T. F. T. Plucknett, *Early English Legal Literature* (Cambridge, 1958), 13.

9. Published as T. F. T. Plucknett, *Statutes and Their Interpretation in the . . . Fourteenth Century* (Cambridge, 1922).

10. He explained the late appearance of discussions of fault on the basis that all early trespass actions were for deliberate wrongs, without asking himself what would happen when an accident victim sued; below, essay 4 at nn. 9, 10. And in connection with the *Humber Ferry Case* he acknowledged a textual correction from "or" to "and not" without altering his translation or realizing that it turned formalistic bickering into a serious legal argument (below, essay 2 at n. 35 for the case, and essay 4, n. 24 for the correction). And there is legal insensitivity in his understanding (*Legislation of Edward I* [Oxford, 1949], 94–95, 104) that the statute *Quia emptores* was only declaratory of a result which had been reached three-quarters of a century earlier; see S. F. C. Milsom, *The Legal Framework of English Feudalism* (Cambridge, 1976), 104, n. 1.

11. For an illustration of this point, see the last of these essays at nn. 57–63. And it is worth observing that S. E. Thorne, the most perceptive historian of the common law since Maitland, made important contributions to our understanding of the law in every century from the twelfth to the seventeenth.

12. Below, essay 4 at nn. 39–43.

13. P. Brand, "Milsom and After," in *The Making of the Common Law* (London and Rio Grande, 1992), 203, esp. at 222–23. Cf. D. W. Sutherland, *The Assize of Novel Disseisin* (Oxford, 1973), esp. at 30–31. Professor Sutherland did, however, agree that the writ was "consciously directed" and "constantly used" against lords; but, similarly equating "disseise" with "dispossess," he did not accept that protection against lords was its original purpose. Cf. below, essay 4 at n. 41, especially on the mention in the writ of the defendant's bailiff.

14. This was Miss Elsie Shanks, who had been working on *Novae Narrationes* for many years. For the Selden Society year book editions were undertaken by other linguists, Miss Dominica Legge and Professor J. P. Collas. The linguistic study had been pioneered by Maitland himself in his first year book volume (17 Selden Society).

15. "Commentary on the Actions" in *Novae Narrationes* (80 Selden Society, 1963).

16. The earliest direct attempt was "Law and Fact in Legal Develop-

ment," 17 *University of Toronto Law Journal* (1967) 1; *Studies in the History of the Common Law* (London and Ronceverte, 1985) 171.

17. Especially in his first two publications, "Not Doing Is No Trespass," [1954] *Cambridge Law Journal* 105 (*Studies* 91) and "Trespass from Henry III to Edward III," 74 *Law Quarterly Review* (1958) 195, 407, 561 (*Studies* 1), and then in his London inaugural lecture, "Reason in the Development of the Common Law," 81 *Law Quarterly Review* (1965) 496 (*Studies* 149). A habit of suspicion toward words may have been formed when doing a fellowship dissertation about the writ of false judgment. *Glanvill* VIII 9 says that if this is found against a lord's court the lord *perpetuo curiam amittet*. This had been taken to mean loss forever of the right to hold a court (Pollock and Maitland, *History of English Law* II:667). But, as in "claims of court," *curia* here means just jurisdiction over the case concerned.

18. As a university law student, on the assumption that he would spend his life with the subject at the bar, he was advised to choose another option. He therefore had to take the bar examination in real property, for which he had the good fortune to be taught together with a future lord chief justice by a future vice-chancellor. But he had a hard time when he came to giving tutorial classes himself, and undertook the radical cure of volunteering to lecture on the subject.

19. It is testimony to the binding force of Maitland's analysis that one crucial point of difference did not dawn on the writer until a quarter of a century later. It is discussed in the fourth of these essays at nn. 82–84.

20. Below, essay 4, n. 40.

21. Published as S. E. Thorne, "English Feudalism and Estates in Land," [1959] *Cambridge Law Journal* 193; reprinted in *Essays in English Legal History* (London and Ronceverte, 1985), 13. One can wonder whether the word *feudalism* itself predisposed historians to dismiss the lecture. Maitland treated feudalism with unaccustomed contempt, S. F. C. Milsom, "Pollock and Maitland: A Lawyer's Retrospect," in *The History of English Law: Centenary Essays on "Pollock and Maitland,"* ed. John Hudson, 89 *Proceedings of the British Academy* (1996), at 246. See also n. 31 below.

22. Below, essay 4, text preceding n. 80.

23. Thorne never seemed so exhilarated as he was at a party after the lecture, and a recollected snatch of conversation may strike a chord with

those who remember his habit of talk: "I think that's got mort d'ancestor right—good old Mort."

24. "How on earth could he have been so excited about that? There's nothing good in it."

25. Pollock and Maitland, *History of English Law* (reissue at 1968) I:lxxxv.

26. S. F. C. Milsom, *Historical Foundations of the Common Law*, 1st ed. (London, 1969). Cf. 2d ed. (London, 1981).

27. S. F. C. Milsom, *The Legal Framework of English Feudalism* (Cambridge, 1976).

28. Ibid., chapter 1.

29. See Milsom, *The Legal Framework*, esp. chapter 3.

30. "Maitland and the Grand Assize" (1995), 7 *Haskins Society Journal* 151 (Woodbridge and Rochester, N.Y., 1997).

31. One teacher of medieval history pushed his certainty to a disdainful conclusion: "The idea of land being held for service is pretty silly, what?" More serious remarks made to the writer suggest that in legal history the gulf between lawyers and historians has been made even wider by the contemporary canons of historical propriety: "How can you hope to cover so long a period?" "How can you talk about feudalism at a time when the word was not in use?" and "Why don't you do it properly—with names?" Since the subject will always attract its few recruits from both sides of the gulf, it has seemed important to be as clear as possible about the nature of this incomprehension, and the writer can only hope his historian friends do not mistake occasional frustration for hostility.

32. Perhaps it was having to struggle through the endless articles about the "origins" of "trespass" and "case"; below, essay 4 at n. 20.

1. MAKING LAW: LAWYERS AND LAYMEN

1. This is the reality behind Sir Henry Maine's famous statement in *Early Law and Custom* (London, 1883), 389, that "substantive law has at first the look of being gradually secreted in the interstices of procedure."

2. *Bracton* ff.99–99b, ed. Thorne II 284.

3. For *Glanvill* the action would in both cases be called "debt"; X 3, X 13, ed. Hall 117, 128. For plea roll clerks and the compilers of registers

of writs this continued to be the case; S. F. C. Milsom, *Historical Foundations of the Common Law*, 2d ed. (London, 1981), 262–65. See also S. F. C. Milsom, *Studies in the History of the Common Law* (London and Ronceverte, 1985), 121–22, 176–79.

4. *Brevia Placitata* (66 Selden Society).

5. *Britton* I xxix 3, ed. F. M. Nichols, 2 vols. (Oxford, 1865), I:157. See also Milsom, *Studies in the History of the Common Law*, 177–78.

6. *Brinkburn Cartulary* (90 Surtees Society) 105 (1299, original record in CP40/127); YBB 8 Edward II (41 Selden Society) 136; 12 and 13 Edward III (Rolls Series) 245; 29 Lib. Ass. pl.28 f.163. A bailee pleaded robbery as early as 1274, but the facts were denied, CP40/5 m.5d.

7. *Coggs* v *Barnard* (1703) 2 Ld. Raym. 909 *per* Holt C.J.

8. YB 20 and 21 Edward I (Rolls Series) 189. The report is reproduced and discussed in F. Pollock and F. W. Maitland, *History of English Law*, 2 vols. (Cambridge, 1898 [1895]), II:180; where it prompted two observations presaging the insight about legal development (above, introduction, n. 3) which came to Maitland when later he turned to editing year books: "We must not be wise above what is written or more precise than the lawyers of the age"; and "Any one who attempts to carry into the reign of Edward I a neat theory about the ownership and possession of movables must be prepared to read elementary lectures on 'general jurisprudence' to the acutest lawyers of that age."

9. This was misunderstood until some sixty years ago, below, essay 4, n. 8.

10. After much deliberation; J. W. Baldwin, "The Intellectual Preparation for the Canon of 1215 Against Ordeals," 36 *Speculum* (1961) 613.

11. The *prison forte et dure* of Stat. Westminster I (1275) c.12 came to be read as *peine forte et dure*. See T. F. T. Plucknett, *Concise History of the Common Law*, 5th ed. (London and Boston, 1956), 125–26.

12. T. A. Green, *Verdict According to Conscience* (Chicago, 1985), 28–64.

13. Stat. 38 Edward III stat.1 c.5 (1364). See generally Plucknett, *Concise History*, 115–16.

14. YB Hil.48 Edward III pl.11 f.6 (1374), translated in J. H. Baker and S. F. C. Milsom, *Sources of English Legal History* (London, 1986), 360–62.

15. For a fuller account of procedural changes in the common law courts and their effect on legal development see Milsom, *Historical Foundations of the Common Law*, chapters 2 and 3.

16. YB 22 Lib.Ass. pl.56 f.98 (1348), translated in Baker and Milsom, *Sources of English Legal History*, 311–12. The case is a particularly dramatic illustration of a plea in confession and avoidance, but there were of course many earlier cases. In 1271, for example, a defendant admitted knocking down the plaintiff's house in order to stop the spread of an urban fire. Milsom, *Studies in the History of the Common Law*, 81.

17. *Select Cases in the Court of King's Bench* I (55 Selden Society) 181.

18. Below at essay 4, n. 70.

19. Below essay 2, nn. 51–53.

20. The absence of earlier discussion was long misunderstood by legal historians, below essay 4 at nn. 9–11.

21. Above, n. 6.

22. See Milsom, *Studies in the History of the Common Law*, 118 and 186.

23. *Anon* (1588) 4 Leonard 81. Cf. below, essay 2, nn. 46, 47.

24. Examples have been collected by Professor Baker; below, essay 2, n. 46.

25. Milsom, *Studies in the History of the Common Law*, 109.

26. The city of London did allow executors to be sued, on the basis that they could swear to the best of their knowledge; *Borough Customs* I (18 Selden Society) 210ff.

27. They were even more important than appears from the present discussion. Undertakings to perform services or to convey land came to be embodied in conditional bonds. The contractor would execute a bond acknowledging his indebtedness to the other party in a good round sum, but this was to be void if the services were done or the conveyance made.

28. Below, essay 2 at n. 57.

29. Below, essay 4 at nn. 9–12.

30. H. F. Jolowicz, "Procedure *in iure* and *apud iudicem*: a Suggestion" in *Atti del Congresso Internationale di Diritto Romano, Bologna II* (1934), 59–81. (I had lost this reference, and am indebted to Professor J. A. Jolowicz for not only finding it but also lending me his father's offprint). Previous explanations of the Roman division had supposed some

fusion of state authority with private arbitration. Jolowicz's suggestion stemmed in part from the English analogy, on which see Milsom, *Studies in the History of the Common Law*, 172.

31. See the introduction at n. 1.

32. Cf. S. F. C. Milsom, "The Past and the Future of Judge-made Law" in *Studies in the History of the Common Law*, 209.

2. CHANGING LAW: FICTIONS AND FORMS

1. On the nature of early custom see below, essay 3 at n. 4.

2. For an example see below, essay 3 at n. 28.

3. T. F. T. Plucknett, *Legislation of Edward I* (Oxford, 1949), 13. The part played by judges in the processes of legislation was also relevant; T. F. T. Plucknett, *Statutes and Their Interpretation in the First Half of the Fourteenth Century* (Cambridge, 1922), 20–25, 49–50.

4. (1677) 29 Charles II c.3. See below at n. 55. The mercantile legislation of Edward I had also been primarily concerned with procedure and proof.

5. *Ancient Law* (London, 1930), 31–36.

6. *The Works of Jeremy Bentham*, ed. J. Bowring (Edinburgh, 1843), 1:243.

7. Stat. 31 Elizabeth I (1589) c.6.

8. Above, essay 1 at nn. 2–7.

9. For *Glanvill* there was only "debt," X 3, ed. Hall 117. For the incomplete separation of the two, see S. F. C. Milsom, *Studies in the History of the Common Law* (London and Ronceverte, 1985), 177.

10. S. F. C. Milsom, *Historical Foundations of the Common Law*, 2d ed. (London, 1981), 271.

11. Below, essay 3, text following n. 16.

12. For a discussion of detinue conceived as a single entity see C. H. S. Fifoot, *History and Sources of the Common Law* (London, 1949), 24ff. When first brought to royal courts, the customary claim of widow or children to a share of a dead man's chattel wealth might also be initiated by the same detinue writ; Milsom, *Historical Foundations of the Common Law*, 270.

13. These essays will use the phrase "forms of action" because it is inseparably associated with this vision of legal development; but the phrase itself is relatively modern. See below at n. 65 and essay 4, n. 25.

14. Other evidence inconsistent with the early primacy of writs appears in S. F. C. Milsom, *Legal Framework of English Feudalism* (Cambridge, 1976), 128 and n. 2: for the same factual complaint the plaintiff might use any one of three different writs, his choice governed by the proof he would offer.

15. The principal year book discussion is YB Trin. 33 Henry VI pl.12 f.26v (1455), where the trover count is described as "a new-found Haliday." This is probably a reference to YB Trin. 29 Edward III f.38v (1355), translated in J. H. Baker and S. F. C. Milsom, *Sources of English Legal History* (London, 1986), 267–69, in which it was agreed that issue could not be taken on the actual steps by which the thing was supposed to have come to the hands of the defendant, whose name was Halyday.

16. Below, at nn. 59–62.

17. YB Hil. 48 Edward III pl.11 f.6 (1374), translated in Baker and Milsom, *Sources of English Legal History*, 360–62, where the argument for allowing wager of law seems for the moment to prevail.

18. R. C. Palmer, *English Law in the Age of the Black Death* (Chapel Hill, 1993).

19. A jury in 1304, apparently worried about process by arrest, tried in vain to say, "Guilty but not with force and arms," YB 32 and 33 Edward I (Rolls Series) 259. Also cited below, n. 56 and essay 4, n. 14.

20. YB 10 Edward II (54 Selden Society) 140.

21. Milsom, *Studies in the History of the Common Law*, 65–67.

22. Ibid., 25–27, especially the explicit writ against a smith at 27. See also *Select Cases of Trespass from the King's Courts 1307–1399* II (103 Selden Society) 261, 262, 262–63, 264.

23. The change was not immediately complete. General *vi et armis* actions continued to be brought against smiths, e.g., the last references in the preceding note.

24. But of course the assertion still offered a handle for lawyers' objections, as with the doctrine that the king's peace died with the king. See Milsom, *Studies in the History of the Common Law*, 74–75.

25. Below, essay 4 at n. 18.

26. Stats. 25 Edward III stat.5 c.17 (1352, *capias* in most personal actions), 19 Henry VII c.9 (1504, in actions on the case).

27. Cf. *Glanvill* X 8, X 18, ed. Hall 124, 132.

28. See J. S. Beckerman, "The Forty-Shilling Jurisdictional Limit in Medieval English Personal Actions," in *Legal History Studies 1972* (Cardiff, 1975), 110–17.

29. Milsom, *Studies in the History of the Common Law*, 106–8.

30. 39s. 11½d; H. M. Cam, *The Hundred and the Hundred Rolls* (London, 1930), 182.

31. Above, essay 1, text following n. 27.

32. Above, at n. 17.

33. Above, at nn. 20–22.

34. *Vieux Natura Brevium*, ed c.1518 f.49v; ed 1584 f.123; see generally Milsom, *Studies in the History of the Common Law*, 7 n. 36, 33–34, 46, 56.

35. YB 22 *Liber assisarum* pl.41 f.94 (1348), translated in Baker and Milsom, *Sources of English Legal History*, 358–59. Cf. below, essay 4, n. 24.

36. *Glanvill* X 14, ed. Hall 129.

37. See generally Milsom, *Studies in the History of the Common Law*, 126–28.

38. See J. H. Baker, *An Introduction to English Legal History*, 4th ed. (London, 2002), 331–33, 355–56.

39. *Derry v. Peek* (1889) 14 App. Cas. 337.

40. Above, at n. 35. For legal historians the clarity was obscured by a mistake in the text as printed in the black-letter year books, below, essay 4, n. 24.

41. On the "forms of action" see above, essay 2, n. 13, below, essay 4, nn. 23–26. Until recently historians saw this formalistic approach as aboriginal, below, at n. 65.

42. Doige's Case (1442), YB Trin. 20 Hen.VI pl.4 f.34, translated in Baker and Milsom, *Sources of English Legal History*, 390–95. The plaintiff started two separate actions, and *Sources* suggests that the later differs from the earlier in making the plaintiff complain expressly that he was defrauded of the land. This is a misreading which the editors regret. In neither action is the plaintiff said to have been defrauded "of" any-

thing specific: he was defrauded by the sale to the third party. See generally, and for the London background in particular, Milsom, *Historical Foundations of the Common Law*, 328ff.

43. The situation of the Inns between Westminster Hall and Guildhall may not be coincidence, and there was a tradition that counsel periodically made themselves available in St. Paul's Cathedral, presumably for city clients.

44. "My word is my bond."

45. Milsom, *Historical Foundations of the Common Law*, 329.

46. J. H. Baker, *The Legal Profession and the Common Law* (London and Ronceverte, 1986), 426 nn. 93, 94.

47. Above, essay 1 at n. 23.

48. *Pykering* v. *Thurgoode* (1532), *Spelman's Reports* I (93 Selden Society) Accion sur le case no. 5, p. 4; record in vol. II (94 Selden Society) 247.

49. J. H. Baker, *Spelman's Reports* II (94 Selden Society) 280; Milsom, *Historical Foundations of the Common Law*, 338.

50. Milsom, ibid.

51. This was exacerbated by the working of the *nisi prius* system: a plaintiff suing in the King's Bench might find the jury being directed by a judge from the Common Pleas.

52. The revealing order of words as between damages and debt is taken from Coke's report, Baker and Milsom, *Sources of English Legal History*, 440.

53. Because the facts were laid out in a special verdict the serious discussions came in *Slade's Case* (1602), for which the principal materials are most readily available in Baker and Milsom, *Sources of English Legal History*, 420–41. Cf. Baker, *The Legal Profession and the Common Law*, 393–432.

54. F. W. Maitland, *Collected Papers* (Cambridge, 1911), 1:447.

55. (1677) 29 Charles II c.3.

56. YB 32 and 33 Edward I (Rolls Series) 259 (1304), also cited above in n. 19 and below, essay 4, n. 14.

57. The part of the judges with fictions was not always so passive. They seem for example eventually to have forced defendants to accept the fictions involved in the action of ejectment; Baker, *An Introduction to English Legal History*, 302.

58. Below, at n. 63.

59. Above, at n. 9.

60. To show that he would not in fact have a remedy in detinue against anyone else either, the plaintiff may assert that the sale was to persons unknown, and arguably he should also assert that the sale was in market overt, so that his "property" was gone and he could not have even a theoretical remedy in detinue for these goods against anyone. See especially *Mounteagle v. Countess of Worcester* (1555) in Baker and Milsom, *Sources of English Legal History*, 531–33.

61. In the earlier actions what was "converted to the defendant's use" was not the actual object but the proceeds of its sale.

62. See *Isaack v. Clark* (1615) 2 Bulstrode 306 (Baker and Milsom, *Sources*, 541).

63. The formulation is that of the third "resolution" in Coke's report of *Slade's Case*, n. 53 above at 439.

64. There have been various misunderstandings, the most serious arising from the assumption that "contract executory" (obligation contracted but not discharged, i.e., unpaid debt) meant the same as our executory contract. See further Baker, *The Legal Profession and the Common Law*, 422.

65. Below, essay 4, text at nn. 18–29.

66. *Consolidated Co. v. Curtis* [1892] 1 QB 495. Cf. the odd dispute in *Oakley v. Lyster* [1931] 1 KB 148.

3. MANAGEMENT, CUSTOM, AND LAW

1. *Vindicatio: "ex jure Quiritium."*

2. Above, essay 1, text between nn. 1 and 8.

3. Above, ibid. at n. 6.

4. Julius Goebel, *Felony and Misdemeanor* (New York, 1937), 229, n. 80 at 231.

5. Land Transfer Act s.1.

6. Pipe Roll 10 John (23 Pipe Roll Society, NS), ed. D. M. Stenton 113, n. 8 (from Chancellor's Roll); F. M. Stenton, *The First Century of English Feudalism*, 2d ed. (Oxford, 1961), 38; I. J. Sanders, *English Baronies* (Oxford, 1960), 64 (Marshwood).

7. Below, at nn. 16, 19. The case is *Rotuli Curiae Regis* I 360. Cf. an earlier case of a surviving brother claiming land because the dead tenant's son was an infant, below, n. 9, and essay 4 at n. 85.

8. Sidney Painter, *The Reign of King John* (Baltimore, 1949), 1–16 (the succession), 85 ("John himself saw to Arthur"); J. C. Holt, "The *Casus Regis*, 1185–1247" in *Colonial England 1066–1215* (London and Rio Grande, 1997), 307–26.

9. *English Lawsuits from William I to Richard I*, I (106 Selden Society) no. 145, p. 118. The case is more fully considered for a historiographical reason in the following essay at n. 85.

10. C. Johnson, ed., *Dialogus de Scaccario* (London, 1950), 94. The king holds not in wardship but as *escaeta cum herede*.

11. Assize of Northampton (1176) c.4, *Stubbs' Select Charters*, ed. H. W. C. Davis, 9th ed. (Oxford, 1946 [1913]), 179–80.

12. S. F. C. Milsom, "Inheritance by Women" in *On the Laws and Customs of England*, ed. M. S. Arnold, T. A. Green, S. A. Scully, S. D. White (Chapel Hill, 1981), 60–89. See also essay 4, below at n. 66.

13. On *se demisit* (or *resignavit* or *se deposuit*) see S. F. C. Milsom, *The Legal Framework of English Feudalism* (Cambridge, 1976), 146–53.

14. G. C. Homans, *English Villagers of the Thirteenth Century* (Cambridge, Mass., 1941; New York, 1960), 145, 214.

15. This was the judgment of peers which in *Magna Carta* his own tenants sought to impose on the king himself. See below, essay 4 at n. 96.

16. Above, n. 7.

17. f.421, ed. Thorne IV 309. The case referred to concerns dower and does not illustrate the general point: *Curia Regis Rolls* XIII 247.

18. Lord Nottingham in *Duke of Norfolk's Case* (1681) 2 Swanston 454 at 460; 79 Selden Society at 908.

19. Above, nn. 7, 16.

20. *Glanvill* VII 1, ed. Hall 70.

21. *Glanvill* VII 1, ed. Hall 72–74. Maitland, thinking in terms of the descent of property and not of the renewable homage relationship, characterizes "lord and heir" as "this quaint doctrine"; F. Pollock and F. W. Maitland, *History of English Law*, 2d ed. (Cambridge, 1898), II:290. Cf. *Bracton's Note Book*, II, p. 54, n. 6: "queer rule."

22. *Glanvill* VII 1, ed. Hall at 70–71.

23. A memorandum presumably emanating from the justices in eyre is

printed in *Curia Regis Rolls* X 259. For the case see *Rolls of the Justices in Eyre for Gloucestershire* 1221–22 . . . (59 Selden Society) no.598.

24. "Statute" of Merton (1236) c.4.

25. *Pace* Maitland. In Pollock and Maitland, *History of English Law*, I:622–23, he makes an imaginary pre-Merton tenant defy resolutions by his lord and his fellow tenants in ten lines of emotional speech. But this result was due not to ancient "individualism *in excelsis*" but to the assize of novel disseisin.

26. Above, n. 23.

27. There is a partial exception in the mercantile legislation of Edward I, which was however essentially concerned with jurisdictional and procedural difficulties.

28. T. F. T. Plucknett, *Legislation of Edward I* (Oxford, 1949), 106, 108–09.

29. Westminster II (1285) c.1.

30. Cf. the reception by historians of S. E. Thorne's 1959 lecture "English Feudalism and Estates in Land," *Essays in English Legal History* (London and Ronceverte, 1985), 13–29. On their seeming incomprehension of the lecturer's point see above, introduction, at nn. 21–25, and also S. F. C. Milsom, "Pollock and Maitland: A Lawyer's Retrospect" in *The History of English Law: Centenary Essays on "Pollock and Maitland,"* ed. John Hudson, 89 *Proceedings of the British Academy* (1996), at 255.

31. This is the point of the overlooked action *de homagio capiendo*. See S. F. C. Milsom, "Maitland and the Grand Assize" in 7 *Haskins Society Journal* (1997), at 152–53.

32. Above, at n. 19.

33. Milsom, *The Legal Framework of English Feudalism*, 143.

34. The common recovery became a tissue of fiction; but, as with the fictions considered in the preceding essay, it can only have grown from a naturally occurring situation, namely that the original settlor had entailed land to which he was not entitled.

4. HISTORY AND LOST ASSUMPTIONS

1. Legal history is equally not served by the further extreme to which this orthodoxy has been taken, namely concentration on individuals whose

names have come to occupy most or all of the indexes of historians' books. An index of names is not a useful starting point for a historian who is concerned with individual people only if they exemplify a situation which at the time was raising problems for others in similar situations. The first need is to find the situations, not the people.

2. Below, text at nn. 57–63.

3. A relatively modern example is the working of the "post-trial motions," the principal vehicle of legal discussion for more than three centuries and the mechanism which enabled that discussion to take place after the facts had been found. (The motion for a new trial, below at n. 12, was particularly important in the history of tort law). The learning simply became obsolete, and later appreciation of its significance, largely begun in S. F. C. Milsom, *Historical Foundations of the Common Law*, 1st ed. (London, 1969), would have been hard had it not been for the publication in 1929 of a course of lectures at the Inns of Court mainly intended to enable law students of the time to understand pre-Judicature-Act cases; R. Sutton, *Personal Actions at Common Law* (London, 1929).

4. For early English legal history a relevant example is the tendency to assume that a fair picture can be got from the surviving evidence, overwhelmingly from royal or ecclesiastical institutions, without allowing for the part played by early feudal courts which left no records beyond what can be gleaned from charters; cf. F. M. Stenton, *The First Century of English Feudalism*, 2d ed. (Oxford, 1961), 42–83.

5. Above, essay 1 at n. 9.

6. It is likely that suspicion of the neighborhood might often point to one suspected not, e.g., of a particular theft but of being a "common thief."

7. *Glanvill* XIV 2, ed. Hall 173, on concealment of treasure trove. Cf. *Curia Regis Rolls* I 91.

8. N. D. Hurnard, "The Jury of Presentment and the Assize of Clarendon," 56 *English Historical Review* (1941) 374.

9. There was of course evidence, but the assumptions of lawyers at the time made it inconspicuous and the assumptions of historians passed it over, e.g., *Gibbon v. Pepper* (1695), J. H. Baker and S. F. C. Milsom, *Sources of English Legal History* (London, 1986), 335 at 337 nn. 5, 6.

10. T. F. T. Plucknett, *Concise History of the Common Law*, 5th ed. (London, 1956), 465–66.

11. Above, essay 1, text following n. 12.

12. Milsom, *Historical Foundations of the Common Law*, 70–81.

13. Above, essay 2, text between nn. 16 and 25.

14. In YB 32 and 33 Edward I (Rolls Series) 259 (1304) a jury did try to say, "Guilty but not with force and arms," but in vain. The case is cited in essay 2, nn. 19 and 56.

15. For such an explicit writ see S. F. C. Milsom, *Studies in the History of the Common Law* (London and Ronceverte, 1985), 27. For a clear statement of the repugnancy argument see YB 5 Edward II (31 Selden Society) 215 (1312), especially the record of an action for taking with force and arms a document handed to the defendant to inspect.

16. R. C. Palmer, *English Law in the Age of the Black Death* (Chapel Hill, 1993), sees not procedural adjustments but changes of large governmental policy.

17. For a case as early as 1307, but in which the plaintiff claimed to have been hindered while on the king's service, see *Select Cases in the Court of King's Bench*, III (58 Selden Society) 179.

18. Cf. M. J. Prichard, "Trespass, Case, and the Rule in *Williams* v. *Holland*," [1964] *Cambridge Law Journal* 234.

19. Stat. Westminster II c.24.

20. Most of this literature is summarized in C. H. S. Fifoot, *History and Sources of the Common Law* (London, 1949), 44–56 (on origin of trespass), 66–78 (on development of actions on the case).

21. Stat. Gloucester c.8.

22. S. F. C. Milsom, "Not Doing Is No Trespass" (1954) reprinted in *Studies in the History of the Common Law*, 91–103, and "Trespass from Henry III to Edward III" (1958), ibid. 1–90. The sense of "trespass" in local courts was remarked by Glanville Williams, *Liability for Animals* (Cambridge, 1939), 128.

23. Cf. F. Pollock and F. W. Maitland, *History of English Law*, 2d ed. (Cambridge, 1898), II:561: "They are—we say it without scruple—living things. . . . The struggle for life is keen among them and only the fittest survive."

24. For a particularly striking example see Plucknett, *Concise History of the Common Law*, 470. The *Humber Ferry Case* (above, essay 2 at n. 35) is discussed and translated (from the black-letter vulgate) and the

defendant is made to argue that the plaintiff should be suing in "covenant or trespass." A courteous footnote acknowledges the kindness of a correspondent who had sent manuscript readings showing that the black-letter "or" should be "rather than" or "and not": but the significance of this is missed, and neither the translation nor the discussion was altered.

25. The vision gained currency from the posthumous publication of lectures by F. W. Maitland which he had not intended to be published, *The Forms of Action at Common Law* (Cambridge, 1936; originally published in 1909 in the same volume with his lectures on *Equity*). The phrase "forms of action" (adopted in these essays, but with the inverted commas) has probably lent definition and authority to this line of thought. But it came into serious use only in the nineteenth century: actual discussion had been just of propriety as between actions, e.g., "assumpsit" and "debt." The vision was closely associated with the belief that the original writs were the sources from which all common law actions sprang; that belief was similarly associated with the belief that writs represented concepts, above, essay 2, nn. 13, 65, below, n. 35.

26. "We must keep up the boundaries of actions, otherwise we shall introduce the utmost confusion," *Reynolds* v. *Clarke* (1725) *per* Raymond CJ as reported in 1 Strange 634. The question was whether trespass or case was appropriate on the facts.

27. The narrow sense is already discernible in Stat. 19 Henry VII c.9 (1504) providing that the same process (i.e. by *capias*) was to be had in "actions upon the case" as in "actions of trespass or debt." But of course the broad sense survived longer, not only for laymen ("forgive us our trespasses") but also as a generic term for lawyers; see, e.g., the cases of 1610 and 1632 printed in Baker and Milsom, *Sources of English Legal History*, 351, 352. There was also a knock-on effect on the language of the criminal law: offenses less than felony which had been known as "trespasses" became "misdemeanors."

28. Above, essay 2, text following n. 65.

29. Maitland, *The Forms of Action*, 7–9.

30. Including a substantial book: F. Joüon des Longrais, *La conception anglaise de la saisine* (Paris, 1924).

31. The guardian in chivalry has been little discussed, partly because more obviously unfamiliar and partly because the effect of the Assize of

Northampton, c.4 in giving seisin to the infant heir has sometimes been overlooked; see e.g. T. F. T. Plucknett, *Legislation of Edward I* (Oxford, 1949), 81–82.

32. "Ownership and Possession" is the title of his chapter discussing property in land and chattels; Pollock and Maitland, *History of English Law*, II:1–183.

33. F. W. Maitland, *Collected Papers* (Cambridge, 1911), I:358 at 362.

34. Ibid. at 365. Cf. ibid. 370: there is "another side to the picture. . . . He who is seised, though he has no title to the seisin, can alienate the land . . . and his heir shall inherit."

35. Even this is not true of the writ of right of dower, which claims only a life estate (and is addressed to the dead husband's heir as "lord" of whom the widow claims to hold). That writ, and its positioning in early registers as just one of the variant forms of the writ patent telling lords to do right, itself shows that "right" had not started with any connotations like those of "ownership." For another case in which misunderstanding arose from the assumption that a writ was more than just a practical order and somehow represented a concept, see the discussion of detinue, above, essay 2, nn. 8–16.

36. Pollock and Maitland, *History of English Law*, II:46: "English law both medieval and modern seems to accept to the full this theory:— Every title to land has its root in seisin; the title which has its root in the oldest seisin is the best title."

37. Maitland, *Collected Papers*, I:407–57.

38. Difficulties latent in this view are suggested in S. F. C. Milsom, "Maitland and the Grand Assize," 7 *Haskins Society Journal* (1997) 151–77 at 165.

39. A view still sometimes held, although discredited more than sixty years ago; S. E. Thorne, "Livery of Seisin" (1936) in *Essays in English Legal History* (London and Ronceverte, 1985), 31 at 44: "to say that Henry deliberately set out to protect possession in order to deprive the baronial courts of their jurisdiction is completely to misunderstand the conditions of the time."

40. The process, evidenced by previously unnoticed cases on the earliest plea rolls in which a lord being sued in novel disseisin relies on the due process of his court, is described in S. F. C. Milsom, *The Legal Frame-*

work of English Feudalism (Cambridge, 1976), 8ff. A related matter is the far-reaching power which *Glanvill* says a lord could exercise over his tenant in his own court without royal writ; Milsom, "Maitland and the Grand Assize," at 165ff. This was also unnoticed, no doubt because *Glanvill's* statements are not brought together but scattered; and that in turn must be because this power was an assumed feature of his world, barely relevant to the working of the king's court with which he was exclusively concerned. Maitland never mentions either the power or the enforcement process.

41. Historians have objected that any lord had a bailiff. Of course. But see S. F. C. Milsom, "A Lawyer's Retrospect" in *The History of English Law: Centenary Essays on "Pollock and Maitland"* 89 *Proceedings of the British Academy* 243 at 256–57. From the plea rolls it is clear that persons answering as "bailiff" are increasingly just informal representatives (the defendant in novel disseisin could not make an attorney) and also that orders to put back the chattels disappear, being replaced by the award of damages; Milsom, *The Legal Framework of English Feudalism*, 12–13.

42. Pollock and Maitland, *History of English Law*, II:52.

43. Above, n. 40. These cases, in which the defendant makes an express exception to the assize on the ground that he acted by due process of his court, are all from the manorial level and concern free peasant tenements. There is no telling how often the same facts lie behind a general verdict in the assize; Milsom, *The Legal Framework of English Feudalism*, 14–17. No express exceptions have been found concerning higher levels of tenure, where such enforcement may have become rare, but it was not unknown. In 1200 the holder of a knight's fee resists a claim for tenurial dues by his lord on the ground that he has been disseised by the earl of Clare; this disseisin, which is attested by the earl's steward, was for a failure of tenurial duty owed by the lord to the earl as overlord; *Curia Regis Rolls* I 177–78. Cf. Milsom, ibid., 24–25.

44. "English law for six centuries and more will rue this youthful flirtation with Romanism"; Pollock and Maitland, *History of English Law*, II:115. The analogy with the usufructuary came from *Bracton* ff.167b–68, 220–20b, ed. Thorne, III 33, 161–62.

45. *Bracton* f.163, ed. Thorne III 22.

46. *Collected Papers*, I:383.

47. The late Derek Hall used to say that if you found yourself answering a question in terms of "our silly old ancestors" you could be sure you had misunderstood the matter.

48. Above, nn. 40, 43, below, at nn. 95–98.

49. Above, essay 3, nn. 7, 16.

50. Maitland, *Collected Papers*, I:329–57.

51. Cf. Joüon des Longrais, *La conception anglaise* (above, n. 30) at 45: "une jouissance toute pénétrée d'éléments de droit . . . et ne s'en distingue pas dans sa nature."

52. Pollock and Maitland, *History of English Law*, II:38; cf. II:35–36 (unfree tenant seised in lord's court, not in king's). Cf. Thorne, "Livery of Seisin" (above, n. 39) at 43–44.

53. Maitland, *Collected Papers*, I:365.

54. R. Van Caenegem, *Royal Writs* (77 Selden Society) 265.

55. Milsom, *The Legal Framework of English Feudalism*, 18–21.

56. Cf. Plucknett's view that all early actions for trespass *vi et armis* were for deliberate wrongs, above, n. 10.

57. Westminster II (1285) c.21; cf. Gloucester (1278) c.4.

58. There was a dogma that one acting within his fee could not be breaking the king's peace. See S. F. C. Milsom, *Historical Foundations of the Common Law*, 2d ed. (London, 1981), 154 n. 2.

59. Public justice had previously been available to the tenant only when his lord had refused gage and pledge, an offense seen as striking at the established order; *Bracton* f.217b, ed. Thorne III 154: "where gages and pledges fail, peace fails."

60. P. Brand, *The Making of the Common Law* (London and Rio Grande, 1992), 288–92, 319–20.

61. On which see S. F. C. Milsom in *Novae Narrationes* (80 Selden Society) lx.

62. Stat. Westminster II c.2.

63. *Glanvill* IX 1, ed. Hall 104–05. *Glanvill*'s statements about the powers of lords' courts over the tenure of their tenants without royal writ have been overlooked by historians (including Maitland) for reasons suggested above, n. 40.

64. Above, n. 46.

65. *Bracton* ff.29b, 30, ed. Thorne II 99, 100.

66. Above, essay 3, text following n. 12.

67. Such glimpses as the plea rolls give us are in cases in which after a general verdict the loser secures a "certification" by which the assize justices and the recognitors are brought to rehearse the business before the bench or *coram rege*. For a particularly instructive example see S. F. C. Milsom, "What Was a Right of Entry?" [2002] *Cambridge Law Journal* 561 at 571.

68. "Consuetudines diuersarum curiarum" in *Select Cases of Procedure without Writ* (60 Selden Society) cxcv–cciii at cxcix–cc.

69. The only exception mentioned in these essays was that of a lord resisting novel disseisin on the ground that he acted by due process of his court; above, n. 43. Failure to enrol unsuccessful exceptions caused later difficulty; Stat. Westminster II (1285) c.31.

70. In novel disseisin, especially when rights of entry were in issue, a general verdict might require a conclusion on difficult questions of law; and the hardship of making recognitors swear under the threat of attaint came to be recognized in 1285 when statute allowed them to insist on a special verdict, Westminster II c.30.

71. *Bracton's Note Book* no. 1792, translated in Baker and Milsom, *Sources of English Legal History*, 33, and discussed in Milsom, "What Was a Right of Entry?" at 566.

72. D. W. Sutherland, *The Assize of Novel Disseisin* (Oxford, 1973), 108.

73. Milsom, *The Legal Framework of English Feudalism*, 47, 92–93.

74. On *Quia emptores* (1290) see below, text at nn. 90–93. Cf. *De viris religiosis* (1279) and Provisions of Westminster (1259) c.14.

75. Milsom, "Maitland and the Grand Assize," 172 and n. 86.

76. Maitland's account concentrated upon a particular writ, very rarely used and having a history of which he could not have known, which indeed developed from assizes of novel disseisin frustrated by the death of a party. The great majority of writs of entry concerned defective or spent grants. See Milsom, "Maitland and the Grand Assize," 170–75 and the references there cited.

77. Substitutions might be achieved by fine (originally no doubt made in the lord's own court and evidenced by charters), but all ordinary "private" grants were by subinfeudation; Pollock and Maitland, *History of*

English Law, I:345. Cf. Milsom, *The Legal Framework of English Feudalism*, 153.

78. Milsom, *The Legal Framework of English Feudalism*, 88–102.

79. Above, nn. 71, 68.

80. YBB 20 and 21 Edward I (Rolls Series) 8–10; 33–35 Edward I (Rolls Series) 52–54. These cases are discussed in Milsom, "What Was a Right of Entry?" 573.

81. Milsom, *The Legal Framework of English Feudalism*, 54–60.

82. Pollock and Maitland, *History of English Law*, II:46, quoted above, n. 36.

83. New introduction to the 1968 edition of "Pollock and Maitland," *History of English Law*, I:xxvii–xlix; the particular mistake is at xxxi.

84. Milsom, "Maitland and the Grand Assize," 158.

85. *English Lawsuits from William I to Richard I*, I (106 Selden Society) no. 145, p. 118. The brother tried to hold over when the infant came of age (ibid.) and meanwhile to render less than the service due (no. 164, pp. 133–34). He made his request in the king's court, perhaps knowing that the abbot was unwilling; so here the superior jurisdiction was being asked to intervene against the usual custom. The case (also mentioned in essay 3 above at n. 9) should be compared with those in the preceding essay of the incapable elder son (above, essay 3, nn. 7, 16, 19) and the alleged "better knight" (above, essay 3, n. 6).

86. *Glanvill* VII 10, ed. Hall 84.

87. S. F. C. Milsom, "The Origin of Prerogative Wardship" in *Law and Government in Medieval England and Normandy*, ed G. Garnett and J. Hudson (Cambridge, 1994), 223–44, at 226 n. 9.

88. Ibid., last note.

89. The same grammatical dogma with a possessive adjective raised an unnecessary doubt for the translator in *Glanvill* VII 3, ed. Hall 76, n. 2. And the adjectives can obstruct understanding for the grammatical reason as well as by their range of meanings (above, essay 3, text between nn. 1 and 2). In c.3 of the "Coronation Charter" *cum terra sua* is taken by some medievalists as in itself proving that at the time of Henry I an heiress in wardship was herself immediately owner of the inheritance.

90. It has also been thought that the services were invulnerable because the lord could always distrain on chattels within his fee, even if they be-

longed to a subtenant; Plucknett, *Legislation of Edward I*, 102. But this may not always have been so: there is reason to think that distress began as process to enforce what was seen as a personal obligation on the immediate tenant; Milsom, *The Legal Framework of English Feudalism*, 113.

91. "Machinations," Plucknett, *Legislation of Edward I*, 102.

92. Above, essay 3, text at nn. 9–11.

93. In *Bracton* ff.45b–46, ed. Thorne II 141, the writer seems to take malicious pleasure in noting that what the lord bargained for was not the incidents but the services, "so let him take what is his and be gone."

94. Above, text at nn. 38–39.

95. Above, essay 3, text following n. 16.

96. 1215 c.39 (1225 c.29).

97. Cf. J. E. A. Jolliffe, *Angevin Kingship*, 2d ed (London, 1963), esp. at 50–86; J. C. Holt, *Magna Carta*, 2d ed (Cambridge, 1992), esp. at 81–83.

98. Mort d'ancestor and the Assize of Northampton, by permitting an undoubted heir to go in or stay in before satisfying the lord for his relief and the like, had a similar effect on the perception of inheritance; S. E. Thorne, "English Feudalism and Estates in Land" (1959) in *Essays in English Legal History* (London and Ronceverte, 1985), 13–29 at 21–22.

99. As well as the oddity of trial in the House of Lords there were of course other contexts in which "peers" continued to be relevant, especially the process of amercement; *Magna Carta* 1215 c.21 (1225 c.14). The appointed barons of the exchequer, whose title survived until 1881, may first have been so called to make them peers of the real barons who had to be amerced in the exchequer.

100. Holt, *Magna Carta*, 328; more particular usages are surveyed at 75–76. An older book on the Charter, less concerned with its political background and more with its actual words, does pick out the position of tenants in their lords' courts (but does not refer to the "disciplinary" powers of those courts); W. S. McKechnie, *Magna Carta*, 2d ed. (Glasgow, 1914), 377–79.

INDEX

In case any readers may wish to follow up technical points, this index sometimes uses terms of art that do not appear as such in the text, e.g., *De son tort demesne.*

88, 126*n*41; consequences, 89,
94, 104–5, 106; damages in,
126*n*41; due process and, 89,
106; effect on enforcement
of services, 94–95; effect on
perception of tenure, 106;
exception by lord of due
process, 88, 126*n*43; exceptions
in, 97, 128*n*69; extension of,
92–93; general verdict, 97,
126*n*43, 128*n*67; "possessory"
remedy, xxi, xxvi, xxvii, 87;
rights of entry and, 86, 97;
supposed Roman model, 87

Oaths, testing of, 6
Ordeal, 6–7, 77
Ownership and: English land law,
xxiv, 63; inheritance, xxiv, 57;
planning law, 71; Roman law,
52; social and economic structure, 89; tenure, 89, 106; "the
right," 89–90; writs of right,
xxvi, 86, 87, 125*n*35

Painter, S., 120*n*8
Palmer, R. C., 116*n*18, 123*n*16
Part payment of debt, 16–17
Peers: amercement by, 130*n*99;
judgment of, 61, 106
Peine forte et dure, 113*n*11
Perpetuities, Rule against, 65–66
Pleading: in English and Roman
law, 20–21; illustration of,
11–12
Plucknett, T. F. T., on: early legisla-
tion, 115*n*3; fault in trespass,

110*n*10, 122*n*10, 127*n*56;
Humber Ferry Case, 110*n*10,
123–24*n*24; lawyers and legal
history, xix–xx; questions of
law, 110*n*10; *Quia emptores*,
110*n*10, 129–30*n*90, 130*n*91;
wardship and seisin, 124–25*n*31
Possessive adjectives, 52, 54–55,
129*n*89
Possessory claims, xxvi, xxvii, 87,
105
Post-trial motions, 15, 79, 122*n*3
Pound, R., xx
Prerogative wardship, 103
Prescription, 28, 52
Prichard, M. J., 123*n*18
Primogeniture, 58, 66
Promissory estoppel, 39
Property: inherent mischief, 63;
and obligation, 52
Pykering v. Thurgoode, 118*n*48

Relief, 103
Remainders, 66, 73
Rent Acts, xix
Replevin in lords' courts, 94–95
Rescission: breach of warranty,
for, 38, 117*n*36; London, in, 40
Rights of entry, 86, 88, 97–100
Roman law: chosen by other
societies, 20; formulary system,
21, 22; influence on English
law, xiv, 1–2; intellectual
coherence, 20–21; and leaseholder, 88, 126*n*44; and novel
disseisin, 87; procedural division
of lawsuits, 20, 114–15*n*30;